MIKE SPENCER M.A. (HONS.), DIP. TCHG.

LET THE PEOPLE REJOICE

An Interactive History of Christian Music

Ark House Press
PO Box 1722, Port Orchard, WA 98366 USA
PO Box 1321, Mona Vale NSW 1660 Australia
PO Box 318 334, West Harbour, Auckland 0661 New Zealand
arkhousepress.com

Cataloguing in Publication Data:
Title: Let the People Rejoice
ISBN: 9780648371977
Subjects: Christian music;
Other Authors/Contributors: Spencer, Mike

Design by initiateagency.com

Follow Mike Spencer on www.mikespencer.com.au.

Praise the Lord, praise the Lord, let the earth hear his voice!
Praise the Lord, praise the Lord, let the people rejoice!
O come to the Father through Jesus the Son,
and give him the glory, great things he hath done.
Fanny Crosby

CONTENTS

*This book is dedicated to
my talented wife, Christine (Chrissie),
who shares my love for the Lord
and for Christian music.*

FOREWORD

Hymns or choruses? Anthems or modern songs? Should there be a conflict when we consider how the pioneers in Christian music down through the centuries have expressed their praise and worship in the musical genre of their times? From liturgical to Hillsong style worship, each genre has its appointed time and place. Do we understand the heart of those composers and poets who brought amazing and timely expressions of appreciation and worship to the great God of the ages?

Some have written histories of various hymn writers in the past. Mike Spencer has not only done that, but has included an amazing array of interactive music available to the downloader. Now you can read about the hymns and songs while accessing examples on your computer.

Mike's book will be a valuable resource to me, as a Christian programmer on a weekly radio show, providing information and enabling me to track songs through the interactive menus. His smooth flow of sacred music history is very readable, not merely as a resource for study, but also as a pleasant excursion into the past. You will be fascinated by the unfolding of history, up to today's Contemporary Christian Music genre.

I heartily recommend this book to all lovers of the development of Christian music. It honours those many hundreds of composers who were inspired to write by the Holy Spirit.

David Evans
Producer of the weekly Heart and
Soul Radio program in Australia

PREFACE

Let the People Rejoice had its origins in a series of lectures given in a local church in New Zealand, over a period of about five years. The lectures were very well received, and it was felt that the material was valuable enough to form the basis for this present work.

The book is not a complete history of Christian music worldwide. Such an effort would require a large set of encyclopaedias. Rather, it is an attempt to give a broad overview of the main events and trends in the history of Christian music from the book of Genesis through to the present day.

Some Christians may be offended by the fact that I have dealt only cursorily with, or – horrors – not even mentioned, their favourite recording artist or group. Obviously, to mention everyone would be logistically impossible in the context of this book. Certain key songs, song-writers and performers are highlighted because of their exceptional contribution to the development of the genre.

I make no apology for not taking sides in the so-called "worship wars" of recent years. Obviously there are strengths and weaknesses on both sides of the debate, but that is beyond the scope of this book. I have grown up with hymns, gospel songs, praise choruses, songs of the Spirit and Contemporary Christian Music. I love singing them all, and I believe that they all have a valid role to play in our worship services.

This is an interactive book. This means that the reader is invited to interact with the content of the book by accessing certain songs, and either singing them or viewing them on websites such as YouTube.

This symbol means that the reader is invited to listen to or watch a particular song or singer. YouTube is the recommended website for carrying out this task.

This symbol means that the reader is invited to sing or play the song. The words and music can be accessed from a standard hymnal, or from one of a number of websites on the computer. Public Domain songs are available free of charge from websites such as *www.hymnary.org, www.pdhymns.com*, or *library.timelesstruths.org*. Music for other songs will need to be purchased from websites such as *www.musicnotes.com*. Lyrics and guitar chords can usually be accessed free of charge.

INTRODUCTION

"Give me the making of the songs of a nation," said the eighteenth-century Scottish political thinker, Andrew Fletcher, "and I care not who writes its laws."[1] This statement clearly illustrates the effect that music has upon the affairs of a nation. Music can stir the emotions, raise the passions, soothe the sorrows, cheer the weary heart, inspire the intellect, and unite the people as one for a common cause.

The power and diversity of music should not surprise us. The Bible makes it quite clear that music originated in the very heart of the Creator God. There are more than 500 references to music in the Bible.

God's Creation is described as being musical in Isaiah 44:23:

> Sing, O ye heavens; for the LORD hath done it: shout, ye lower parts of the earth: break forth into singing, ye mountains, O forest, and every tree therein: for the LORD hath redeemed Jacob, and glorified himself in Israel.

God Himself is said to be musical in Zephaniah 3:17:

> The LORD thy God in the midst of thee is mighty; he will save, he will rejoice over thee with joy; he will rest in his love, he will joy over thee with singing.

---

[1] Quoted in Ravi Zacharias, *Can Man Live Without God?* Thomas Nelson, Nashville, 1994, p.3.

Some believe that, prior to his controversy with God and subsequent fall, Lucifer (Satan) was the heavenly choirmaster[2]. When he fell, Lucifer did not forfeit his music ministry, but he corrupted it.

This conflict between good and evil, between the music of God's Kingdom and Satan's kingdom has been ongoing throughout the course of history.

There are numerous examples, in the Bible, of music being used for good. For example, in 2 Chronicles 20, we read that that God-ordained praise and worship was instrumental in gaining the victory in battle.

> [21]And when [Jehoshaphat] had consulted with the people, he appointed singers unto the LORD, and that should praise the beauty of holiness, as they went out before the army, and to say, Praise the LORD; for his mercy endureth for ever.

> [22]And when they began to sing and to praise, the LORD set ambushments against the children of Ammon, Moab, and mount Seir, which were come against Judah; and they were smitten.

In 1 Samuel 16:23, music was used to soothe King Saul's mental torment.

> And it came to pass, when the evil spirit from God was upon Saul, that David took an harp, and played with his hand: so Saul was refreshed, and was well, and the evil spirit departed from him.

In Acts 16, when Paul and Silas sang in prison, God not only opened the prison doors, but also saved the jailer and his entire family.

---

[2]   This view is based on a reading of Ezekiel 28:13 in the King James Version.

Thus we can see that the positive effects of music include the bringing of freedom from bondage, victory in battle, healing and salvation. These are powerful spiritual principles that need to be a normal part of our daily Christian walk.

On the other hand, when Moses and Joshua were descending Mount Sinai, after having received God's Commandments on tables of stone, they heard a noise, which Joshua assumed was the noise of battle. Moses, however, knew by revelation that the Israelites had corrupted themselves and were singing and dancing as they worshipped an idol (Exodus 32:18).

We do not have to look very far in today's society to see the role of music and dancing in idol worship.

A useful way to look at music is to compare the three parts of man – spirit, soul and body,[3] with the three elements of music – melody, harmony and rhythm. The following chart illustrates the relationship.

	Basic Parts of Music	Basic Drives in Music	Tension/ Relaxation	Basic Effects of Imbalance
SPIRIT	MELODY To dominate	Spiritual Drive	Rise/ Fall	Tension, unfulfillment, frustration, passion, depression, despair
SOUL	HARMONY To support the melody	Psychological Drive	Dissonance/ Consonance	Confusion, rebellion, pride, sentimentality
BODY	RHYTHM To be concealed in the harmony and subordinate to the melody	Physical Drive	Repetition/ Variation	Sensuality, distraction

From Kevin J. Connor, *The Tabernacle of David*, Bible Temple – Conner Publications, Portland, 1976, p. 180.

---

[3]   1 Thessalonians 5:23

The melody corresponds to the spirit and should generally be dominant. In Ephesians 5:18-19 we read:

> [18]And be not drunk with wine, wherein is excess; but be filled with the Spirit;

> [19]Speaking to yourselves in psalms and hymns and spiritual songs, singing and making melody in your heart to the Lord.

The harmony, which corresponds to the mind and emotions, is secondary and should support the melody.

Rhythm, on the other hand, corresponds to the body. In 1 Corinthians 9:27, Paul relates how he keeps his body in subjection. In the same way, the rhythm should be subordinated to the melody.

Rhythm is essential in music, but we should remember that in a symphony orchestra, while there may be a hundred instruments playing, only three or four are primarily dedicated to rhythm. In many modern rock bands, the reverse is true, with the music being composed almost entirely of rhythm (beat).

> For if ye live after the flesh, ye shall die: but if ye through the Spirit do mortify [put to death] the deeds of the body, ye shall live. (Romans 8:13)

In this book, we will study the history of music in the church, from Bible times right through to the present day. We will study the relationship between music and some of the great events in church history. We will note the controversies that have arisen regarding the use of music in the church, and we will look into the lives of some of the great men and women of God who have contributed to our rich musical heritage.

CHAPTER ONE

MUSIC IN THE BIBLE

In his book, *The Sound of Light*, Don Cusic points out that music had eight functions in the Bible. It was used:

(1) in religious services,
(2) in secular celebrations,
(3) in wars,
(4) as private prayer,
(5) as a means of offering thanksgiving and praise to God,
(6) to record events,
(7) in apocalyptic visions of the final days of earth,
(8) and in visions of life in heaven where songs will be used as a way to honour God with praise and thanksgiving, expressing awe and wonder.[4]

It is interesting that the first mention of musical instruments in the Bible is in a secular context. We are told, in Genesis 4:21, that Jubal (pron. yoo-bawl) "was the father of all such as handle the harp (*kinnor*) and organ (*ugab* – pron. oo gawb)." The word *ugab* is only mentioned four times in the Bible, and it probably refers to a long, transverse flute. Some recent commentators, with some support from such sources as Josephus and Philo (first century A.D.), suggest that Jubal was not the *inventor* of the instruments themselves, but rather the *teacher* of those who "played" (i.e., "handled" in a *bad* sense) these instruments. In other

---

4   Don Cusic, *The Sound of Light*, Hal Leonard Corporation, Milwaukee, 2002, p.1.

words, Jubal was the first before the Flood to *misuse* musical instruments, using their power to move men's minds toward ends that were displeasing to the Lord.

The first mention of singing in the Bible is also in a secular context. In Genesis 31:26-27 we read that Laban pursued Jacob and Rachel and enquired as to why they had left him without the customary farewell involving the use of songs, tabrets and harps. Singing and the playing of musical instruments was obviously well-established in the various Middle Eastern cultures by this stage (estimated to be about 1900 BC).

The first mention of singing in a religious context is in Exodus 15. Moses, the first acknowledged songwriter in the Bible, leads the Israelites in thanksgiving for deliverance from Pharaoh's army that had perished in the waters of the Red Sea. Miriam then leads the women with timbrels and dancing. The word "timbrel" here is the same Hebrew word (*toph*) that was previously translated "tabret." The *toph* was actually a small hand drum, shaped like a tambourine, but without the metal jingles.

A second song written by Moses, under the prompting of the Holy Spirit, is recorded in Deuteronomy 32. The purpose of this song was to remind the Israelites of the way in which God had delivered them from slavery. It also served as a warning as to what would happen should they turn away to worshipping other gods, which, of course, God foreknew would happen (Deuteronomy 31:19-21)

In various places in the Old Testament, God commanded the Israelites to worship Him with singing, praising, shouting and all kinds of musical instruments. Of the actual music that was played we have no record at all. There have been attempts, most notably by the French composer Suzanne Haik-Vantoura (1912 – 2000), to interpret the accents of the Hebrew Scripture as a type of musical notation, but these are by no means universally accepted amongst scholars.[5]

---

[5]   Suzanne Haik-Vantoura, *Music of the Bible Revealed*, 1976.

The Tabernacle of David

The use of music in praise and worship reached a pinnacle during the reign of King David. 1 Chronicles 15 and 16 describe how David established the ministry of singers and musicians to bring up the ark. This ministry became consolidated in the Tabernacle of David, as described in 1 Chronicles 23 - 25. Some 4000 Levites praised the Lord with the instruments David had made (23:5). Of these, 288 were skilled musicians divided into 24 courses, 12 in each course, headed by the 24 sons of Heman, Asaph and Jeduthan. With 24 hours in each day, there was a continual service of praise ascending to God.

Another important ministry of the 4000 Levites was that of "recording." The Psalms, as we know them today were written by many of the Levites, as well as by King David himself. They were written down so that they could be remembered and used in the worship associated with David's Tabernacle.

The word Psalm basically means a sacred song accompanied by a musical instrument. The early Church Fathers used the word "psalter," which comes from the Greek word *psalterion*, meaning a harp or other stringed instrument.

The Talmud does give traditions regarding Psalm singing in the Second Temple. On a sign being given on cymbals, twelve Levites, standing upon the broad step of the stairway leading from the "place of the congregation" to the outer court of the priests, playing upon nine lyres, two harps, and one cymbal, began the singing of the Psalm, while the officiating priests poured out the wine offering.

Younger Levites played other instruments, but did not sing; while the Levitical boys strengthened the treble part by singing and not playing.[6] The pauses of the Psalm, or its divisions, were indicated by blasts of trumpets by priests at the right and left of the cymbalists.

A number of Psalms have been given titles or descriptions, such as "On '*ala-mot*" (Psalm 46), "On the *gittit*" (Psalm 8), "Upon *shoshannim*" (Psalm 45) and "On *machalat*." (Psalm 53). It is suggested that these titles give instruction as to how the Psalm should be performed: "which tune or instruments to use, the musical tempo and emotional context (praise or lament), as well as breathing

---

[6]   Apparently, the singers had to train for five years before being admitted to the choir.

instructions, pauses, and the like."[7] For example, "On '*alamot*" seems to indicate the use of high-pitched voices. Other titles, such as "Sunrise" (Psalm 22 *CJB*), "The Silent Dove in the Distance" (Psalm 56 *CJB*) and "Do Not Destroy" (Psalms 57-59 and 75) may indicate popular tunes to which the Psalms could be sung.

Although the word "Selah" occurs 71 times in the Psalms and 3 times in the book of Habbakuk, the meaning of the word is not altogether clear. In his classic *The Music of the Bible*, John Stainer writes that the word has been variously interpreted as a pause; a repetition; the end of a verse or stanza; a playing with full power (*fortissimo*); a bending of the body and obeisance; or a short, recurring symphony (*ritornello*). Rev. E. Capel Cure believes that Selah indicated a musical interlude during which the musicians would attempt to paint a picture in sound. For example

- The flight or storm Selah (Psalm 55:1-7) involved clapping hands, beating feet, and clashing cymbals. Habbakuk 3:3, 9, 13 is a picture of God coming to save His people in the midst of storms.
- The death knell Selah (Psalm 52:5) depicted judgement, affliction, and death through the use of reed pipes wailing a funeral dirge.
- The sacrificial Selah involved the sound of trumpets accompanying the ritual of the altar, with a blare of silver trumpets blowing, as it were, the sacrificial smoke heavenward. The Selah preceding Psalm 47:5 was the sacrificial interlude of trumpets and loud hallelujahs, which died away as the smoke grew thinner.
- In the war Selah (Psalm 60:4), trumpets - probably shofar - would be used.[8]

In Amos 9:11, the prophet states, "In that day will I raise up the tabernacle of David that is fallen, and close up the breaches thereof; and I will raise up his ruins, and I will build it as in the days of old." James quotes this verse in Acts 15:16, while issuing instructions to the new Gentile converts. While we understand that this verse refers to the Gentiles coming in to New Covenantal blessing, many modern commentators also see it as a foundational text for modern

---

7   Tim Dowley, *Christian Music: A Global History*, Lion Hudson, Oxford, 2011, p. 23.
8   John Stainer, *The Music of the Bible*, Novello and Co. Ltd., 1914 edition, pp. 82 and 90ff.

praise and worship, with the "clapping of hands, lifting of hands, spiritual songs, instruments of worship, spontaneous praise, dancing and rejoicing before the Lord, etc" modelled on the Davidic pattern.[9]

Temple Worship

Davidic worship continued in Solomon's temple. In 2 Chronicles 5:12-14, during the dedication of the temple, we read that 120 priests stood with the Levitical singers and musicians sounding trumpets. They must have made an incredibly inspiring sound. So much so that, in verse 14, as a result of the unity amongst the priests and Levites, and the offering of praise and thanksgiving, the Temple was filled with the presence of the Lord in the form of a cloud. Praise and worship released God's power amongst His people.

John Stainer makes the following observation:

It will not be difficult to form an opinion of the general effect of Temple music on solemn occasions if we know the grand musical results of harps, trumpets, cymbals, and other simple instruments, when used in large numbers simultaneously or in alternating masses.

It is easy to describe it in an off-hand way as *barbarous*. Barbarous in one sense, no doubt, it was; so, too, was the frequent gash of the uplift sacrificial knife in the throat of helpless victims on reeking altars.

Yet the great Jehovah himself condescended to consecrate by His visible presence ceremonials of such sort, and why may we not believe that the sacred fire touched the singers' lips and urged on the cunning fingers of harpists, when songs of praise, mixing with the wreathing smoke of incense, found their way to His throne, the outpourings of true reverence and holy joy?

---

9   Kevin Conner, *Restoration Theology*, KJC Publications, Vermont, Victoria, 1998, pp.212ff.

If one of us could now be transported into the midst of such a scene, an overpowering sense of awe and sublimity would be inevitable. But how much more must the devout Israelites themselves have been affected, who felt that their little band - a mere handful in the midst of mighty heathen nations - was, as it were, the very casket permitted to hold the revelation of God to man, of Creator to His creatures; and could sing in the Psalmist's words which now stir the heart and draw forth the song, how from time to time His mighty hand had strengthened and His loving arm had fenced them?

Let us try and enter into their inmost feelings, when the softest music of their harps wafted the story of His kindness and guidance from side to side of their noble Temple, or a burst of trumpet-sound heralded the recital of His crushing defeat of their enemies, soon again to give place to the chorus leaping from every heart,

Give thanks unto the Lord,
His mercy endureth for ever.

(John Stainer, *The Music of the Bible,* Novello,
Ewer & Co., 1879, pp. 174-175)

Music figured prominently in the revivals of Hezekiah, Josiah, Ezra and Nehemiah. For example, we read in Nehemiah 12:27 that "at the dedication of the wall of Jerusalem they sought the Levites out of all their places, to bring them to Jerusalem, to keep the dedication with gladness, both with thanksgivings, and with singing, with cymbals, psalteries, and with harps."

Since there were no written prayer books, canticles (songs or chants with a Biblical text) were often sung using the call-and-response method. John Arthur Smith suggests that there may have been five ways of performing responsorial canticles during the Second Temple[10] period:

---

[10] The Second Temple was completed around 515 BC, following the return of the Jewish exiles from the Babylonian Captivity. It was substantially enlarged by King Herod the Great and continued to operate until it was destroyed by the Romans in AD 70.

1. The congregation repeats each verse after the leader.
2. The congregation repeats a standard refrain after the leader sings each verse.
3. The congregation completes the second half of a verse after the leader.
4. The leader sings the opening words of the verse and the congregation repeats them and then completes the verse.
5. The leader sings the whole song and the congregation then repeats it.[11]

By the end of the Old Testament era, however, music had degenerated into ritualistic chanting. The joyful songs of Moses, David, Asaph and Solomon were no longer heard.

The Second Jewish Temple. Model in the Israel Museum, 2006.

---

[11] John Arthur Smith, "Musical Aspects of Old Testament Canticles in Their Biblical Setting," in Iain Fenlon, ed., *Early Music*, Vol.17, Cambridge University Press, Cambridge, 1998, pp. 232-35. Quoted in Dowley, *op. cit.*, p. 22

Music in the New Testament

There are not a large number of references to singing or the playing of musical instruments in the New Testament. A key verse, however, which indicates that music still held an important place in Christian worship, is Ephesians 5:19. Here, Paul exhorts the members of the church to speak in "psalms and hymns and spiritual songs, singing and making melody in your heart to the Lord." It would seem that psalms and hymns were songs that were already known, and probably written down, while spiritual songs could be songs sung extemporaneously, "in the spirit."

In Matthew 26:30, we are told that, following the Last Supper, Jesus and His disciples sang a hymn before going out to the Mount of Olives. We do not know what they sang, but it has been suggested that it could have been the Great Hallel or paschal hymn (Psalms 113-118), usually sung after the Passover by the Jews.[12]

The book of Revelation contains several references to songs new and old. For example, Revelation 15:3-5 speaks about the Song of Moses referred to earlier in this book. The allusion here is to the victory gained over Pharaoh at the Red Sea and the power of the deliverance of the Passover Lamb.

---

[12] See, for example, *Fausset's Bible Dictionary*, <http://www.bible-history.com/faussets/H/Hymns>.

CHAPTER TWO

MUSICAL INSTRUMENTS IN THE BIBLE

It is difficult to know what music the ancient Hebrews played or what the instruments they played were like. This is because of the prohibition against painting or sculpture (based on the Second Commandment, Exodus 20:4). Any ideas we have are from coins or from depictions from other cultures. It is highly likely that ancient Hebrew music was influenced by the Egyptian and Babylonian captivities.

Stringed Instruments

1 Chronicles 15:16 refers to three instruments – the *nebel* (or *nevel*), *kinnor* and cymbal. In the King James Version, the *nebel* is translated as psaltery, while the *kinnor* is translated as harp. The same two words are used in Psalm 150:3 - "Praise him with the psaltery (*nebel*) and harp (*kinnor*)."

The *kinnor* was not, in fact, a harp as we know it, but rather a type of portable lyre. The *nebel* is sometimes referred to as a viol. The *nebel* had twelve or more strings, whereas the *kinnor* had eight to ten strings.

In Psalm 33:2, a third instrument is added. This is the *asor* (pronounced awe-sore), a ten-stringed lyre or decachord. "Praise the Lord with *kinnor*: sing unto him with the *nebel* and *asor*."

Three other stringed instruments are of note in the Bible. The *sabeca* (sab-bek-aw') was possible a larger harp, while the *psanterin* (pes-an-tay-reen') was a dulcimer, which is the ancestor of the clavichord, harpsichord (a keyboard in which the strings are plucked, rather than hit) and the pianoforte.

The *kithara* (kee-thaw-roce) was probably a more fully-developed harp. The word guitar comes from *kithara*.

In Daniel 3:5 and 15, a number of instruments are mentioned in association with pagan worship. The instruments are the cornet (*keren*), flute (*mashrokitha*), harp (*kithara*), sackbut (*sabeca* – this is a harp, not a sackbut, which is an early type of trombone)[13], psaltery (*psanterin*), and dulcimer (not a dulcimer, but a *symphonia* or bagpipes). The last three instruments should actually read harp, psaltery or dulcimer, and bagpipes.

A representation of King David playing the *kinnor*.

---

[13]   In many translations, the *sabeca* is called a 'trigon'. This was a small, triangular harp, with four strings. It was held vertically, with its sound-box resting on the player's shoulders.

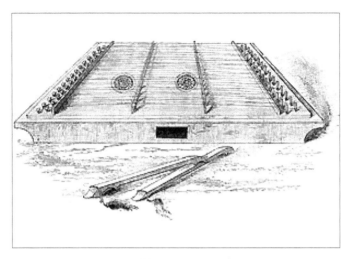

The *psanterin.*

Summary of Stringed Instruments

Kinnor – always translated harp. In fact it is a portable lyre.

Nebel – psaltery or portable harp

Asor – ten-stringed lyre or decachord

Sabeca – larger harp?

Psanterin – dulcimer

Kithara – more fully-developed harp

Wind Instruments

In Matthew 9:23, "Jesus came into the ruler's house, and saw the minstrels and the people making a noise." There had been a death in the family and the pipers had been hired to assist in the mourning. The music would have been soft and melancholy, in contrast to Isaiah 30:29 and 1 Kings 1:40, where the pipes are making a joyful noise.

The Hebrew word is *khalil*, and it means pipe or flute. There is a possibility that it may have been a double pipe. *Harper's Bible Dictionary* states that it "con-

11

sisted of two separate pieces of reed, metal or ivory, each with its own mouth-piece containing either a single (clarinet-type) or double (oboe-type) reed. The pipes were played together, one probably acting as a drone accompaniment."

The *mashrokitha*, which we have already mentioned in Daniel 3, was a flute, while the *keren* (or *qeren*) was probably a cornet or horn made from animal horns. In Joshua 6:5, which describes the capture of Jericho, the word *jobel* (pronounced yo-bale) is added to *keren*, making a *jobel*-horn. Although this has been translated ram's horn in the King James Version, it could also be a jubi-lee-trumpet, used on occasions of great solemnity. The *symphonia*, also men-tioned in Daniel 3, was a primitive form of bagpipes.

In Genesis 4:21, we find the first mention of instruments in the Bible. These are the harp (*kinnor*) and organ (*ugab* - pronounced oo-gawb). It is possible that *ugab* refers to panpipes, but the best evidence suggests that it may have been a long, transverse flute.[14]

Probably the most famous wind instrument used by the ancient Hebrews was the *shofar*. It has been described as a ram's horn, although the horns of other animals were used too. In Joshua 6:5, as well as in other places, it is referred to as a trumpet. It is the only ancient Hebrew instrument that is still in common use in both Jewish and Christian contexts.

The *shofar* was used in both peace and war, in the presence of royalty, as well as during the execution of priestly rites. On New Year's Day (Rosh ha-Shanah, also called the Day or Feast of Trumpets) it was a practice to blow a straight ram's horn with a gold-plated mouthpiece and on the Day of Atonement a curved horn with a silver-plated mouthpiece was used. In later times, following the destruction of Herod's Temple by the Romans in AD 70, the Jews banned the playing of all instruments, apart from the *shofar*, as a sign of mourning.

The *khatsotsrah* (khats-o-tser-aw'), or silver trumpet, is also associated with the Feast of Trumpets. The two trumpets described in Numbers 10:2 were used to assemble the people. If both trumpets were sounded, then the whole camp would assemble. If only one trumpet was sounded, then only the princes would assemble.

---

[14] Dowley, *op. cit.*, p. 19.

1 Chronicles 15:28 describes how David brought up the Ark of the Covenant to be placed in his Tabernacle. "Thus all Israel brought up the ark of the covenant of the Lord with shouting, and with the sound of the *shofar*, and with *khatsotsrah*, and with *metsiltayim*, making a noise with *nebel* and *kinnor*."

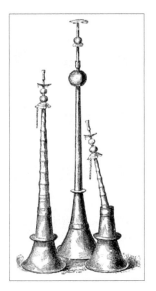

Khatsotsrah (silver trumpets)

Summary of Wind Instruments
Khalil – pipe (possibly a double pipe)
Mashrokitha – flute
Ugab – long, transverse flute
Symphonia - bagpipes
Keren – cornet or horn
Shofar – ram's horn
Khatsotsrah – silver trumpet

Percussion Instruments

Percussion instruments were not widely used in Bible times, probably because of their association with pagan religious rituals. The only percussion instruments allowed to accompany psalm-singing were the cymbals (cf. 1 Chronicles 25:1), which were always used in pairs.

In the accounts relating to the transport of the Ark of the Covenant, the cymbals are called either *metsiltayim* (1 Chronicles 15:16) or *tsiltsilim* (2 Samuel 6:5). The former are explicitly said to have been made of bronze. Psalm 150:5 apparently refers to two types of cymbals with different tone or resonance qualities (and therefore different sizes or shapes).

1 Corinthians 13:1 speaks of two musical instruments – the "sounding brass" and the "tinkling cymbal" (KJV). Paul is warning the Corinthians that their vocal spiritual gifts, although they may sound wonderful, are worthless if they are not tempered with love.

The Greek word for brass is *chalkos* (khal-kos). Some interpret this as a gong, but a clearer picture of what Paul is referring to may come from the thought that "sounding brass" may refer to the large brass vases that were put at the back of Greek theatres to amplify the actors' voices.

The "tinkling cymbal" is *kumbalon*. Stainer comments, "inasmuch as they give out a shrill and clanging sound, and are incapable of being tempered or tuned so as to form ever-varied chords with those musical instruments which surround it, they too well illustrate the hollowness and emptiness of character which, while making noble professions with the tongue, lacks that gift of charity which, if it truly glowed in us all, would soon attune all the discords of this world into such a sweet harmony as were worthy of heaven itself."[15]

There are four more percussion instruments. The *toph* (hand drum) has already been mentioned in Chapter One. The *menaaneim*, which is translated cornet in 2 Samuel 6:5, was more likely to have been a sistrum. A sistrum was a U-shaped metal frame on a handle, with movable cross-bars that rattled when shaken. It was not primarily associated with the Jewish culture, and is only mentioned once in the Bible. Likewise, the *shalishim* is only mentioned once, in 1

---

[15]   John Stainer, *The Music of the Bible*, Novello, Ewer & Co., 1879, p.142.

Samuel 18:6, where it is translated as "instruments of music." The word derives from the number three, and may be referring to a triangle, or even a three-stringed lyre, which would make it a stringed instrument. The drum (*tympana*) is first mentioned in Hebrew in the Book of the Maccabees.

Phaghamon were bells attached to the high priest's robe They are only mentioned twice, in Exodus 28:33-35 and 39:25-26, and are better translated as metal jingles, since true bells were not used in that period of Israel's history. The high priest was commanded by the Lord, on pain of death, to wear these "bells" while ministering in the Holy Place (not the Most Holy Place).[16]

A sistrum

---

[16] Most scholars believe that the story of the High Priest wearing a rope around his ankle so that he could be dragged out of the Most Holy Place, if he were to drop dead in the presence of the Lord, is actually mythical, as there is no reference to any such practice in ancient documents.

Summary of Percussion Instruments
Metsiltayim – cymbal
Tsiltsilim – cymbal
Kumbalon – cymbal
Phaghamon – bells – metal jinglers
Menaaneim - sistrum
Shalishim – triangle?
Toph – hand drum

Psalm 150
1 Praise ye the LORD. Praise God in his sanctuary: praise him in the firmament of his power.
2 Praise him for his mighty acts: praise him according to his excellent greatness.
3 Praise him with the sound of the *shofar:* praise him with the *nebel* and *kinnor.*
4 Praise him with the *toph* and dance: praise him with stringed instruments and *ugab.*
5 Praise him upon the loud *tsiltsilim* praise him upon the high sounding *tsiltsilim.*
6 Let every thing that hath breath praise the LORD. Praise ye the LORD.

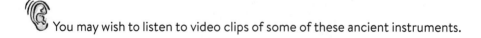 You may wish to listen to video clips of some of these ancient instruments.

CHAPTER THREE

SINGING IN
THE EARLY CHURCH

As we have already seen, in Chapter One, Paul exhorts the members of the church to speak in "psalms and hymns and spiritual songs, singing and making melody in your heart to the Lord" (Ephesians 5:19)

Psalm singing in the early Christian church was of three types –

1. Direct psalmody involved singing the entire Psalm without modification.
2. Responsorial psalmody was taken from the Jewish synagogue. The entire song would be sung by a soloist while a choir, or the congregation, would respond with short exclamations, such as "Amen" or "Alleluia."
3. Antiphonal psalmody means "opposite voice," and refers to the call and response type of singing. A piece of music would be performed by two semi-independent choirs or half-choirs interacting with one another, often singing alternate musical phrases.[17]

Eusebius, Bishop of Caesarea (AD 263-339) believed that "The command to sing psalms is in force in all churches which exist among the nations, not only for the Greeks but also for the Barbarians . . ."

---

[17]　See, for example, *Encyclopaedia Britannica*, <http://www.britannica.com/art/psalmody>.

A "hymn" has been defined as "a lyric poem, reverently and devotionally conceived, which is designed to be sung and which expresses the worshipper's attitude toward God or God's purposes in human life. It should be simple and metrical in form, genuinely emotional, poetic and literary in style, spiritual in quality, and in its ideas so direct and so immediately apparent as to unify a congregation while singing it."[18]

The earliest known Christian hymns, or canticles, are the Song of Mary, as set forth in Luke 1:46-55 (also known as the *Magnificat*), Zechariah's hymn of rejoicing in Luke 1:68-79 (the *Benedictus*), the angels' chorus in Luke 2:14 (*Gloria in excelsis*), and Simeon's song in Luke 2:29-32 (the *Nunc dimittis*). We do not know what tunes were used for these hymns. Paul's exaltation in 1 Timothy 1:17, set to music, contains phrases that would have been familiar to both Jewish ("the King of the ages") and Greek ("for ever and ever") believers.

In time, Christians began to write their own spiritual songs, in line with Apostolic teaching. In Ephesians 5:14b, Paul quotes from an existing source, possibly a Greek baptismal chant, or a song about Christ's resurrection. The three lines "Awake thou that sleepest, and arise from the dead, and Christ shall give thee light" may have been "the first lines of a responsorial song, led by the president and answered by the church," or a "chorus that the congregation chanted in response to verses sung solo by the worship leader."[19]

In the post-Apostolic era, the early church fathers had various attitudes towards music.[20]

- Ignatius of Antioch (AD 35-110) used the metaphor of monophonic singing to encourage Christians in their love for Christ:

Therefore by your concord and harmonious love Jesus Christ is being sung. Now all of you together become a choir so that being harmoniously

---

[18] Harry Askew and Hugh MacElrath, *Sing with Understanding: An Introduction to Christian Hymnology*, Broadman Press, Nashville, 1980.

[19] Dowley, *op.cit.*, p. 32.

[20] See Kevin J.Conner, *The Tabernacle of David*, Bible Temple – Conner Publications, Portland, 1976, pp. 122-123.

in concord and receiving the key note from God in unison you may sing with one voice through Jesus Christ to the Father.

- Tertullian (AD 155-240) offered details of worship in his North African community:

After manual ablution, and the bringing in of lights, each is asked to stand forth and sing, as he can, a hymn to God, either one from the Holy Scriptures or one of his own composing . . .

Tertullian

- Clement of Alexandria (AD 150-220) wrote many hymns but condemned the use of instruments because of their association with pagan rituals.
- During the third century AD, controversy arose over whether it was permissible to sing humanly-composed hymns, or whether only the Psalms of David should be used in worship. This was a controversy that was to continue right through the Middle Ages

- John Chrysostom (AD 354-407) taught that there was no need for instruments or trained voices. The New Testament "instrument" was the true song that came from the heart of the worshipper.
- Jerome (AD 340-420) warned against turning the house of God into a theatre.
- The Council of Laodicea (probably AD 363-364) passed a regulation that "psalms composed by private men must not be used in the church." It also ruled that none should sing in the church except regularly appointed singers. This was apparently done to ensure the highest standards of singing.

The earliest known Christian hymnal is *Odes of Solomon*. The 42 odes were collated by a Jewish Christian, possibly an Essene[21], about 125 AD. The hymnal was written in Syriac, a similar language to Aramaic. The title, *Odes of Solomon*, may indicate that the hymns were written in the tradition of Solomon's writings, or that they were written by a person using the pen name "Solomon."

Ode 10

1. The Lord has directed my mouth by His Word, and has opened my heart by His Light.
2. And He has caused to dwell in me His immortal life, and permitted me to proclaim the fruit of His peace.
3. To convert the lives of those who desire to come to Him, and to lead those who are captive into freedom.
4. I took courage and became strong and captured the world, and the captivity became mine for the glory of the Most High, and of God my Father.

---

[21] The Essenes were a Jewish sect that lived a communal lifestyle dedicated to asceticism and voluntary poverty.

5. And the Gentiles who had been dispersed were gathered together, but I was not defiled by my love for them, because they had praised me in high places.
6. And the traces of light were set upon their heart, and they walked according to my life and were saved, and they became my people forever and ever.

Hallelujah.

Ode 13

1. Behold, the Lord is our mirror. Open your eyes and see them in Him.
2. And learn the manner of your face, then declare praises to His Spirit.
3. And wipe the paint from your face, and love His holiness and put it on.
4. Then you will be unblemished at all times with Him.

Hallelujah.

Translation by James H. Charlesworth

The oldest Christian hymn that has been discovered with both words and musical notes dates from the late third century AD. It is known as the Oxyrhynchus Hymn, because it was found on the back of a papyrus near the Egyptian city of Oxyrhynchus in 1918. It is also sometimes called the "Hymn to the Holy Trinity."

Oxyrhynchus Hymn

Oxyrhynchus Hymn

Oxyrhyncus Hymn

Let it be silent
Let the Luminous stars not shine,
Let the winds (?) and all the noisy rivers die down;
And as we hymn the Father, the Son and the Holy Spirit,
Let all the powers add "Amen Amen"
Empire, praise always, and glory to God,
The sole giver of good things, Amen Amen."

Translation by M. L. West

Another hymn, of Greek origin, was recorded in the fourth century AD, although it is believed to be much older. Called *Phos Hilaron* ("Gladdening Light"), it is still sung in the Eastern Orthodox Church when the evening lamp is lit:

Having come to the setting of the sun
And seeing the evening light,
We hymn the Father, the Son and the Holy Spirit of God

CHAPTER FOUR

THE MIDDLE AGES

The controversy surrounding Christian music, which had begun during the Post-Apostolic era, continued throughout the thousand-year period known as the Middle Ages. It focused on three issues in particular:

1. Which musical instruments, if any, should be used in worship?
2. Should singing be done only by trained singers, or should the whole congregation participate?
3. Should only Psalms be sung, or was it acceptable to sing humanly-composed hymns?

By the fourth century AD, worship had become formalised into a liturgy, or set order of service, with the Mass (communion) as the high point. A shift had taken place from a people-centred to a clergy-centred and controlled service.

This, of course, greatly impacted the music that was used. There was a reaction against the multiple instruments and metrical music of secular circuses and theatres. Church music was to centre on vocal melody of a more mystical nature. Priestly liturgical chant replaced congregational singing.

The "cathedral office," as it was called, became a pattern for worship throughout the church. In the morning, Psalms 51 and 63, and especially Psalms 148-50 were used, while in the evening, Psalm 105 was in common use. In the

Eastern church, Psalm 141 was used in the evening, along with the ancient Greek hymn *Phos hilaron*.[22]

In addition, the Greek expressions *Kyrie eleison* ("Lord have mercy") and *Christe eleison* ("Christ have mercy") were retained as congregational responses in the Latin litany (petitions spoken or chanted by a priest or deacon as a form of prayer).

The canticles (scriptural texts) described earlier were retained throughout the Middle Ages, and new ones were added, including the *Gloria Patri* ("Glory to the Father . . ."), *Sanctus* ("holy" – based on Isaiah 6:3), and *Benedictus qui venit* ("Blessed is he who comes in the name of the Lord").

Hymns of the Early Middle Ages

Despite the prohibition on singing all non-Biblical texts, imposed by the Council of Laodicea, Christian hymns continued to be written and sung in churches. Bishop Ambrose of Milan (c. AD 337-397) encouraged congregational singing and wrote many hymns. He believed that hymns were a valuable method of teaching theology. Two of his hymns that are still sung today are "O Splendour of God's Glory Bright," and "Saviour of the Nations, Come." This latter sung was originally translated from Latin by Martin Luther.

---

[22] The formal split between the Roman Catholic Church and the Eastern Orthodox Churches took place in AD 1054.

An early mosaic of Ambrose of Milan

 Watch "Hymn History O Splendour of God's Glory Bright" on YouTube

Other hymn-writers of the time include Hilary of Poitiers (c. 315-366), Venantius Fortunatus (c. 540-601), and Aurelius Prudentius Clemens (c. 348-410). Prudentius grew up in Spain and became a lawyer and a judge. In 379 he became part of the Christian emperor's staff in Rome, but left in 395 to enter a monastery. Here he wrote a number of hymns, two of which are "Of the Father's Love Begotten" and "Earth Has Many a Noble City."

 Watch "Hymn History Of the Father's Love Begotten" on YouTube

The hymn *Te Deum* has been put to music by many different composers. It is still used in the Catholic Church and in some Anglican, Methodist and Lutheran Churches. The title comes from the opening Latin words *Te Deum laudamus* ("Thee, O God, We Praise").

Christian Chant

Christian chant is basically "a Latin text sung in unison to a simple melody."[23] Tonally, it often takes an arch shape, starting low, rising high and then falling back down again. Pure chant, which is often called "plainsong," gets its name from the fact that the text and melody are unencumbered by harmonies, instrumental accompaniment, rhythm or accents.

Chanting was practised in the Jewish Temple and in the synagogues, as a means of remembering Scripture, and it was passed on to the early church. When Christianity became legal in the Roman Empire, and great churches and basilicas were built, chanting had the practical advantage of making the readings audible to the congregation.

The chants and liturgies of the West originally varied from place to place, but they eventually coalesced into a centralised Roman liturgical practice known as Gregorian Chant.

Pope Gregory I (590 –604) was a key figure in this movement. Tradition has it that Gregorian Chants are named after him, but some scholars believe that they developed later – in the early 700s - and may have been named after Pope Gregory I as a marketing device to give them respectable credentials. In 1903, Pope Pius X wrote "the Gregorian Chant has always been regarded as the peculiar heritage of the Catholic Church, and therefore a type of music that is her very own – regarded as the supreme model for sacred music."[24] He also forbade accompaniment by piano and "all noisy or irreverent instruments such as drums, kettledrums, cymbals, triangles, and so on . . ."

One of the most famous Gregorian Chants is called *Veni Creator Spiritus* ("Come Creator Spirit"). It is performed during the liturgical celebration of the feast of Pentecost. It is also sung at occasions such as the entrance of Cardinals

---

[23]   Dowley, *op. cit.*, p. 50. Chanting is a form of monophony, a single melodic line without accompaniment. Homophony, on the other hand, is a line of melody supported by chords. Most hymns use homophony.

[24]   *Tra Le Solecitudini*, or *Instruction on Sacred Music.* was a *Motu Proprio* (Papal Edict) promulgated by the pope on November 22, 1903. See, for example <https://adoremus.org/1903/11/22/tra-le-sollecitudini>.

to the Sistine Chapel to elect a new pope, as well as the consecration of bishops, the ordination of priests, the dedication of churches, the celebration of synods or councils, the coronation of kings and other solemn events. The hymn is also widely used in the Anglican Church.

Before the invention of modern musical staff notation, inflective marks were used to indicate the general shape of the music, but not the rhythm. These marks, known as *neumes*, indicated a melodic block, or a group of notes to be applied to a text.

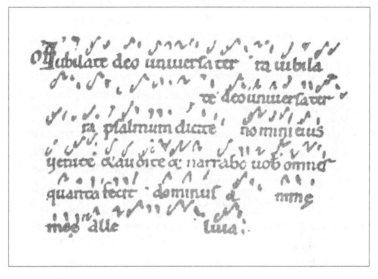

Cheironomic *neumes* applied to the chant *Jubilate deo universa terra* in the ninth century. Cheironomic *neumes* are thought to imitate hand gestures, as in conducting.

By the thirteenth century, a system of square notation was in use on a four-lined staff. Groups of squares or diamonds indicated ascending or descending tones. This system of *neumes* was standardised by the monks of the Benedictine abbey at Solesmes in the nineteenth century. It is still used today in modern chant books.

Watch a version of the Gregorian Chant *Veni Creator Spiritus* that shows the square notation.

Tropes and sequences originated in the eighth or ninth century. Both were embellishments to the existing liturgy, but whereas tropes were introductions, insertions, or additions that had no meaning when separated from the liturgical text, sequences were independent units – often popular tunes of the time – that were inserted into chant settings. Many famous sequences were composed, including *Veni Sanctus Spiritus* ("Come, Holy Spirit") and *Dies irea* ("Day of Wrath"). *Veni Sanctus Spiritus* has been attributed to both Pope Innocent III and Archbishop Stephen Langton of Canterbury.

Listen to a version of *Dies irea* (Gregorian Chant)

Tropes provided the basis for dramatised presentations of parts of the Gospel story. The angels' question to the women at Jesus' tomb "Whom do you seek?" *(Quem quaeritis)* – a trope from the Easter Mass – was one of the first of many liturgical dramas that eventually spread out from the church to the marketplace. "From the little trope *Quem quaeritis* we can trace the rebirth of theatre – even musical theatre – in Western Europe.[25]

---

[25] Dowley, *op.cit.*, p. 60.

Hildegard of Bingen ("Sibyl of the Rhine") (1098 – 1179)

Hildegard receiving a vision and dictating it to her secretary.

Hildegard's parents dedicated her to the church at a young age. She received her education at the Benedictine monastery of Disibodenberg and joined the convent as a teenager. Later, she took over the leadership as prioress, and went on to found another two convents at Rupertsburg and Eibingen.

She recorded 26 prophetic visions in a work entitled *Scivias* ("Know the Ways of the Lord"). Some of these visions refer to end-time events. She also wrote on natural science, practised healing, and corresponded with bishops, popes and kings.

She is perhaps most well known for her music. Unlike contemporary chants, which had a very narrow tonal range, Hildegard's music encompassed over two and a half octaves. More than 70 of her works were included in a collection called *Symphonia armonie celestium revelationum* ("Symphony of the Harmony of Heavenly Revelations"). Her *Ordo Virtutum* ("Play of the Virtues") is a liturgical drama, probably written around 1151.

"Hildegard theorized that music represents the symphony of angels praising God, the balanced proportions of the revolving celestial spheres, the weaving together of body and soul, and the concealed designs of nature."[26]

 Listen to music by Hidegard of Bingen

Hymns of the Later Middle Ages

Bernard of Clairvaux (1091 – 1153)

An idealised portrait of Bernard of Clairvaux.

Despite a general move away from the use of hymns composed by "private men," there were still those within the Church who wrote songs, some beautiful and profound.

---

[26]   *Ibid.*, p. 63.

Bernard was born in Burgundy, France. He became a famous monk, theologian, scholar, preacher and poet. His father, Tesselin, was a brave knight, but it was his mother, Aletta, who had the greatest influence upon him. She consecrated him to God from his birth, and, at the age of 22, he entered the small Cistercian monastery at Citeaux. Later he was sent to found a monastery in the Valley of Wormwood, which he renamed Clairvaux.

His strict discipline and ascetic lifestyle probably contributed to the ill-health that plagued him all his life. However, he became very well-known and his advice was much sort after by both kings and popes. Altogether he founded 163 monasteries throughout Europe.

His life was pure and his spiritual vitality strong. He had a great love for Jesus and gloried in the Cross. In a controversy with a fellow scholar who claimed that Christ did not die to pay the penalty for sin, but rather to demonstrate God's love, Bernard replied, "I was made a sinner by deriving my being from Adam; I am made just by being washed in the blood of Christ and not by Christ's 'words and example'." The great Reformer, Martin Luther, called Bernard "the best monk that ever lived, whom I admire beyond all the rest put together."

Bernard wrote many hymns, some of which are still sung today.

 "Jesus, the Very Thought of Thee"

St. Francis of Assisi (1181/1182 – 1226)

St. Francis of Assisi (Attributed to Cimabue)

Saint Francis was born Giovanni Francesco di Bernardone in Assisi, Italy, in 1182. After an early indulgent life as a soldier, he reformed his ways dramatically, at the age of twenty-five, and determined to serve God by imitating the selfless life of Christ in all that he did. Although his family were people of considerable means, Francis scorned the possession of material goods, denounced his inherited wealth, denied himself everything but the most meagre necessities, and devoted himself completely to moving about his area as Christ's representative. At the age of twenty-eight Francis founded the influential Franciscan Order of Friars, which developed into a large movement of young men and some women who adopted his religious beliefs and ascetic style of life.

Throughout his life Saint Francis made much use of singing and believed strongly in the importance of church music. In all, he wrote more than sixty hymns for use in the monastery.

The so-called "Prayer of St. Francis" is often sung today under the title "Lord, Make Me an Instrument of Thy Peace." The origin of this song cannot be traced beyond the year 1912, so although the words doubtless express the sentiments of St. Francis, it is unlikely that he actually wrote it.

On the other hand, he did write a hymn known as the "Canticle of the Sun," which, in a paraphrased form, has become one of the great hymns of the Christian church – "All Creatures of Our God and King." The English translation was made by William Draper, a village rector in England, who prepared the hymn for a children's choir festival at some time between 1899 and 1919. The tune that is used for this hymn first appeared in a Roman Catholic hymnal in Cologne, Germany, in 1623.

 "All Creatures of Our God and King"

Canticle of the Sun (English translation)

Most high, all powerful, all good Lord!
All praise is Yours, all glory, all honour, and all blessing.
To You, alone, Most High, do they belong.
No mortal lips are worthy to pronounce Your name.
Be praised, my Lord, through all Your creatures,
especially through my lord Brother Sun,
who brings the day; and You give light through him.
And he is beautiful and radiant in all his splendour!
Of You, Most High, he bears the likeness.
Be praised, my Lord, through Sister Moon and the stars;
in the heavens You have made them bright, precious and beautiful.
Be praised, my Lord, through Brothers Wind and Air,
and clouds and storms, and all the weather,
through which You give Your creatures sustenance.
Be praised, my Lord, through Sister Water;
she is very useful, and humble, and precious, and pure.

Be praised, my Lord, through Brother Fire,
through whom You brighten the night.
He is beautiful and cheerful, and powerful and strong.
Be praised, my Lord, through our sister Mother Earth,
who feeds us and rules us,
and produces various fruits with coloured flowers and herbs.
Be praised, my Lord, through those who forgive for love of You;
through those who endure sickness and trial.
Happy those who endure in peace,
for by You, Most High, they will be crowned.
Be praised, my Lord, through our sister Bodily Death,
from whose embrace no living person can escape.
Woe to those who die in mortal sin!
Happy those she finds doing Your most holy will.
The second death can do no harm to them.
Praise and bless my Lord, and give thanks,
and serve Him with great humility.
Translated by Bill Barrett from the Umbrian text of the *Assisi codex*.

"O Come O Come Emmanuel"

"O Come O Come Emmanuel" is another hymn that is still commonly sung, especially at Christmas time. It finds its origin in the medieval Roman Church of the twelfth century and possibly even earlier. It began as a series of Antiphons - short statements sung at the beginning of the Psalm or Canticle at Vespers during the Advent season. Each of the Antiphons greets the Saviour with one of the many titles ascribed to Him in the Scriptures: Emmanuel, Lord of Might, Rod of Jesse, Day-Spring, Key of David. The melody for this text was originally a Chant, possibly used by Franciscan nuns in the fifteenth century. Thomas Helmore adapted this chant tune and published it in 1856 in his *Hymnal Noted, Part II*. The words were translated from Latin to English by John Neale, 1851, in his *Medieval Hymns*.

"O Come O Come Emmanuel"

The Development of Polyphony

No one knows when polyphony (two or more simultaneous lines of independent melody) was first used. Early experiments seem to have culminated in the Notre Dame school of polyphony, in Paris. Polyphonic singing naturally required greater skill, and so the division between the untrained laity and the clergy widened. As singing became more complex, some commentators, such as twelfth-century Bishop of Chartres, John of Salisbury, criticised it as more performance than worship – a frequently recurring comment about Christian music right down to the present day!

The new type of music was aided by Guido of Arezzo's invention of modern musical staff notation in the early eleventh century. The new notation did not indicate timing, and most of the early polyphonic songs – known as *organum* – were sung in triple time, as a sign of respect to the Trinity.

Organum featured two identical parallel lines of melody, in fourths or fifths or even octaves, sung together. Thirds and sixths could also be used, as they introduced an interesting dissonant sound. "Florid organum" featured a singer, or the congregation, singing a slow chant (the *cantus firmus*), while another singer sang a more varied or ornamental part. The first singer eventually became known as a "tenor," from the Latin word *tenere*, "to hold down." By the twelfth century, lines of melody were operating more independently, and moving about freely, in true contrapuntal style.[27]

Listen to an example of early parallel *organum*. You can also watch "Evolving Chant into Organum to Florid Organum."

---

27   In polyphony, the horizontal flow of the various melodies is more important than the vertical, or harmonic, structure typical of homophony.

These developments required refinements of the musical notation system to enable it to depict rhythm. In the middle of the thirteenth century, Franco of Cologne (c.1240 – 1280) developed a system of musical notation where the duration of the note was determined by its appearance on the page and not from context alone. His work *Ars cantuis mensurabilis* ("The Art of Measuring Music") formed the basis for our modern Western system of semibreves, minims and crotchets.

Two of the earliest composers of true polyphonic music were Léonin (c. 1159 – 1201) and Pérotin (c. 1170 – 1206). They were both possibly associated with the Notre Dame school of polyphony, as was Franco of Cologne. Some of the works of both composers are contained in the *Magnus Liber Organi* ("The Great Book of Organum"). Pérotin added a third and sometimes a fourth part to his *organum*, with the parts being sung in contrapuntal style.

Pérotin's *Viderunt omnes*, ca. 13th century.

Listen to Pérotin's *Viderunt omnes* ("All the Ends of the Earth Have Seen the Salvation of Our God")

CHAPTER FIVE

RENAISSANCE AND REFORMATION

The Renaissance

The Renaissance ("Rebirth") was the period between 1350 and 1650 in which occurred a "rebirth" of culture and learning. In Southern Europe, led by Italy, the emphasis was on returning to the (pagan) Greek and Roman classics; in the North, the Holy Bible in the original Greek and Hebrew was the main source of enlightenment.

Of course, musicians and composers had no Greek or Roman music to refer back to, so they were able to innovate. In an early example of "cross-over," many composers wrote both secular and sacred music. In addition, popular songs were sometimes used as the basis for a church mass. A popular example of this was the French folksong, *L'Homme arme* ("The Armed Man"), which was used over and over again in religious contexts.

The polyphonic mass and the Renaissance motet were the two main types of sacred music composed at this time. The mass had five or six movements – the *Kyrie, Gloria, Credo, Sanctus* (sometimes with a separate *Benedictus)*, and *Agnus Dei*. The Renaissance motet was a standalone piece of polyphonic music set to the words of Scripture or the liturgy.

The Renaissance choir typically consisted of four parts – soprano, alto, tenor and bass – similar to today, with the exception that the soprano part was sung by young boys rather than women. Musical instruments also began to make an appearance, despite some fierce opposition. The organ was the first instrument to be used, followed by strings, brass, and some small ensembles.

Many of the Renaissance composers of sacred music came from Burgundy, which at that time consisted of parts of the Netherlands, Belgium and northern France. Other composers came from Spain, the Italian states and England.

The three most influential Burgundian composers of the fifteenth and sixteenth centuries were Guillaume Dufay (c.1400 – 1474), Johaness Ockeghem (c. 1410 or 1430 – 1497), and Josquin des Prez (c. 1445 - 1521).

This woodcut of Josquin des Prez is based on an
original oil painting no longer in existence.

Josquin was regarded by many as the greatest composer of his age. In his extensive travels, he absorbed many musical styles. His polyphony is very expressive, and is designed to touch the emotions, unlike the more mathematical music of the Middle Ages.

🎧 Listen to a live performance of Josquin des Prez's *In te Domine speravi* on YouTube.

The Italian composer **Giovanni Pierluigi da Palestrina (c. 1525 – 1594)** spent most of his career working for the church in Rome. At a time when the Council of Trent (1562) was seeking to purify church music, Palestrina's compositions are a "model of clarity, with up to six well-balanced and beautifully harmonized voice parts."[28] The melodies are comfortable to sing, and the words can be easily heard by the listeners (a point made by the Council).

All things should indeed be so ordered that the Masses, whether they be celebrated with or without singing, may reach tranquilly into the ears and hearts of those who hear them, when everything is executed clearly and at the right speed. In the case of those Masses which are celebrated with singing and with organ, let nothing profane be intermingled, but only hymns and divine praises. The whole plan of singing in musical modes should be constituted not to give empty pleasure to the ear, but in such a way that the words may be clearly understood by all, and thus the hearts of listeners be drawn to the desire of heavenly harmonies, in the contemplation of the joys of the blessed. They shall also banish from church all music that contains, whether in the singing or in the organ playing, things that are lascivious or impure.

Council of Trent, September 10, 1562.

🎧 Listen to a live performance of one of the movements from Palestrina's *Missa Papae Marcelli* ("Pope Marcellus Mass") on You Tube.

---

[28] Dowley, *op. cit.*, p. 78.

Thomas Tallis (c. 1505 – 1585) was one of the English Renaissance composers. Writing at a time when the English church was transitioning from Protestantism to Catholicism (under Queen Mary I) and back to Protestantism again (under Queen Elizabeth I), Tallis had to walk something of a tightrope. Although he managed to avoid religious controversy, he and his collaborator, William Byrd, both remained committed Roman Catholics. In 1575, Queen Elizabeth granted Tallis and Byrd a 21-year monopoly for polyphonic music and a patent to print and publish music.

There is no surviving contemporary portrait of Thomas Tallis. This picture was created 150 years after his death and is probably not a true likeness. Engraving by Niccolò Haym after a portrait by Gerard van der Gucht.

Tallis' compositions range from anthems set to English words, such as "If Ye Love Me," through to Latin compositions, including the celebrated forty-part motet *Spem in alium*, written for five eight-part overlapping choirs. A Cambridge Professor of Music, Thomas Tudway, considered this piece of music too complex to be performed.

In 1567, Tallis contributed nine tunes for Archbishop Parker's *Psalter*, a collection of vernacular Psalm settings. The third "Why fum'th in fight" (Psalm 2) became known as the "third mode melody" and was used by Ralph Vaughan Williams as the theme for his 1910 *Fantasia on a Theme of Thomas Tallis*. The tune for the eighth setting, "God grant with grace" (Psalm 67) became known as Tallis' Canon. It was later used by Bishop Thomas Ken (1637 – 1711) for his evening hymn "Glory to Thee, My God, This Night" (also known as "All Praise to Thee, My God, this Night"). The last verse of this hymn, "Praise God from Whom All Blessings Flow," is sung by itself, as a doxology, often to the tune OLD HUNDREDTH.[29]

 Listen to a live performance of *Spem in alium* on YouTube
Listen to, or sing, "If Ye Love Me"
"Glory to Thee, My God, This Night"
You may wish to listen to Ralph Vaughan Williams' *Fantasia on a Theme of Thomas Tallis*

---

[29] "Praise God from Whom All Blessings Flow" is also the last verse of another well-known hymn by Bishop Thomas Ken – "Awake, My Soul, and with the Sun."

"Glory to thee, my God, this night"

Glory to thee, my God, this night,
For all the blessings of the light:
Keep me, O keep me, King of kings,
Beneath thine own almighty wings.

Forgive me, Lord, for thy dear Son,
The ill that I this day have done;
That with the world, myself, and thee,
I, ere I sleep, at peace may be.

O may my soul on thee repose,
And with sweet sleep mine eyelids close;
Sleep that shall me more vigorous make
To serve my God when I awake.

Praise God, from whom all blessings flow;
Praise him, all creatures here below;
Praise him above, ye heavenly host:
Praise Father, Son, and Holy Ghost.

The Reformation

The term Reformation is used to describe the movement to reform abuses within the Roman Catholic Church, which eventually led to a schism and the formation of the various Protestant Churches. The starting year for the Reformation is usually taken as 1517, when Martin Luther posted his *Ninety-Five Theses* on the door of the Castle Church in Wittenberg, Saxony. However, there had been other reforming movements in Europe many years before this event.

Jan Hus (1372-1415)

Jan Hus was a priest and Master at Charles University in Prague. Following the teachings of John Wycliffe of England, he tried to reform the church in Bohemia and Moravia (now the Czech Republic). Hus was burned at the stake for heresy in 1415, but within 100 years, as many as 90 percent of the inhabitants of Bohemia had left the Roman Catholic Church.

Hus wrote a number of hymns, including "Oh, Ye Warriors of the Lord," and "Jesus Christ, Our Blessed Saviour." These were contained in a collection of 89 hymns in the Czech language, published as early as 1504.

The hymn "Fairest Lord Jesus" may also have an association with Jan Hus. It has been called the Crusaders' Hymn, because it was wrongly thought that it was sung by the German Crusaders as they made their way to the Holy Land in the twelfth century.

Jan Hus.

The truth seems to be that the words originated within the Jesuit Order of the Roman Catholic Church, while the tune was used by a small group of Huss's followers, who settled in Silesia (now part of Poland) after they were driven out of Bohemia in the bloody anti-Reformation purge of 1620. The English adaptation, by Richard Storrs Willis, first appeared in his *Church Chorals and Choir Studies* in 1850.

 "Jesus Christ, Our Blessed Saviour"
"Fairest Lord Jesus"

The Moravian Church, with its strong evangelical/missionary emphasis, grew directly out of the Hussite movement. In 1722, the Moravian *Unitas fratrum* ("Unity of Brethren") took shelter from Catholic persecution on the estate of Count Nikolaus von Zinzendorf, in Saxony, founding the town of Hernhut. The Moravians pioneered the modern Protestant missionary movement, sending hundreds of missionaries all over the world.

The Moravians had a special love for music, and this blossomed when the church became established in the American colonies after the mid-1700s. The Moravian church service, known as a *Singstunde*, was composed almost entirely of hymns, with verses from different songs interwoven together to illustrate the theme of the day.

Moravian composers, such as Count Nicolaus von Zinzendorf and Christian Gregor, wrote thousands of songs for their worship services, using musical instruments such as the organ, string orchestras, woodwinds and brasses to accompany the singers. The trombone ensemble *(Posaunenchor)* was a peculiar feature of the Moravian communities.

"Jesus, Lead Thou On" by Count von Zinzendorf
You may wish to listen to a Moravian trombone choir.

Martin Luther (1483 – 1546)

Martin Luther was born on November 10, 1483, in Eisleben, Germany. His father, Hans, was in the copper mining business; and his mother, Margarethe, was a pious Catholic. Both parents were very strict.

Luther studied at the University of Erfurt, receiving his Master's degree in 1505.

One day during a severe thunderstorm, the frightened Luther vowed to St. Anne (the supposed mother of Mary) that he would become a monk if he were not killed with lightning. His father, who wanted him to be a lawyer and make money, was furious; but young Luther kept his vow and entered an Augustinian monastery. Here, he was ordained a priest, saying his first mass in 1507.

In 1508, Luther became professor of theology at the new University of Wittenberg, a position that he held until his death. However, he was shocked, upon visiting Rome in 1510-11, to see the immorality, carnality and greedy luxury of the Catholic Church.

In 1512 at Wittenberg, Luther received his doctorate in theology. As he studied and taught the Scriptures, however, he became increasingly aware of his own sinful state. He tried, without success, to find peace through bodily humiliation. Eventually, as he read Romans 1:17 - "For therein [the gospel of Christ] is the righteousness of God revealed from faith to faith: as it is written, The just shall live by faith" – he realised that a person can only come into right standing with god through faith in Jesus Christ. This doctrine of justification by faith would become the cornerstone of the Reformation.

In 1517, Pope Leo X needed funds for the building of St. Peter's in Rome. To supply this need, the Archbishop of Mainz hired a Dominican monk, John Tetzel, to sell indulgences in Germany. Tetzel promised that people who bought indulgences would be completely forgiven for all their sins. Luther was scandalised. On October 31, 1517, he posted his *Ninety-five Theses*, or topics for debate, upon the door of the Castle Church. October 31 is now known as Reformation Day in Protestant lands and marks the traditional beginning date for the Reformation.

Gradually, Luther began to question and then to reject the authority of the Pope as well as church councils. He became convinced of the supreme authority of the Bible and wrote tracts and books justifying his position from Scripture.

In 1518, Luther was summoned to the Diet (Parliament) of Augsburg where he refused Cardinal Cajetan's demands that he recant. Luther wrote able pamphlets attacking the Roman system in the light of the Bible. The Pope issued a bull declaring Brother Martin a heretic and excommunicating him. Luther's books were burned.

Luther's response was to publicly burn the Pope's decree. With his life now in danger, Luther was protected by his civil ruler, the Elector Frederick of Saxony. After attending the Imperial Diet of Worms in 1521, where he had gallantly defended the faith before the Emperor and his nobles, Luther was kidnapped by friends and taken to safety in Wartburg Castle. Here he translated the New Testament into German.

Returning to Wittenberg in 1522, Luther was disturbed by the extremes to which the Reformation had gone in his absence. In 1525, he refused to give his support to the Peasant Revolt on the grounds that Christians should submit to lawful authority.

In 1525, Luther married Katherine von Bora, an ex-nun who brought much joy to his life. With six children, much music, and constant student guests, the Luther household was a delightful place to visit.

Many of Luther's later years were spent in organizing the church and formalizing the Lutheran doctrinal position. When Catholicism was declared the only legal faith of the German states in 1529, at the second Diet of Speier, the Lutheran rulers "protested." This is the origin of the term Protestant.

The great Reformer died on a trip to Eisleben in 1546.

Much of Luther's success was due to the use of Johann Gutenberg's movable type printing press, which had been invented some time before 1450. Using the printing technology, Luther's followers were able to circulate his writings, not only throughout the German states, but throughout the whole of Europe. Without the printing press, the Reformation would have been much more localised. The printing press also facilitated the widespread distribution of church music and ensured accurate transcription and interpretation.

While Martin Luther's contribution to the Reformation is rightly regarded as pivotal, it is not always recognised that this contribution extended beyond theology and church practice into the realm of music. An accomplished singer and musician (he played the lute and the flute), Luther wrote 37 known hymns, many of which are still sung today. As well as composing his own tunes, he used German folk tunes and popular songs and gave them Christian lyrics.

The German people had already begun to sing Christian songs in their own language, despite the fact that congregational singing in church had been outlawed for the past thousand years. Luther took it much further, declaring, "I intend to make . . . spiritual songs so that the Word of God even by means of song may live among the people."

Luther felt that devotion to the beauty of music positively influenced moral or ethical development. He said, "I am not of the opinion that all arts are to be cast down and destroyed on account of the Gospel, as some fanatics protest; on the other hand I would gladly see all arts, especially music, in the service of Him who has given and created them." Luther believed that music had strong educational and ethical power, so he wanted the entire congregation to participate in the music of the services. In addition, according to Luther, music was one of the primary methods of counteracting the Devil's work.

He made the study of music compulsory in all schools, and a requirement for ordination into the ministry. While he allowed the organ and choir in church, he was not opposed to other instruments being used.

Luther's most famous song (or "chorale") is "A Mighty Fortress is Our God" (*Ein feste Burg ist unser Gott*). In the lines "And though the world, with devils filled, should threaten to undo us; we will not fear for God hath willed, His truth to triumph through us," Luther states his faith in the triumph of the Reformation against the forces of Catholicism and the German state.

In another hymn, "From Depths of Woe I Cry To You" (*Aus tiefer Not schrei ich zu dir*), Luther develops his doctrine of justification by faith alone.

Thy love and grace alone avail
To blot out my transgression;
The best and holiest deeds must fail
To break sin's dread oppression.

"Ein' feste Burg."

Ein feste Burg ist unser Gott with Martin Luther's signature.

Luther compiled a total of nine hymnals, containing Latin hymns, popular religious songs, and secular tunes with Christian lyrics. Among them is the Christmas carol *In dolci jubilo* ("Good Christian Men, Rejoice"), which is thought to have been composed by the German mystic, Heinrich Seuse, around 1328. The chorale *Nun komm, der Heiden Heiland* ("Saviour of the Nations, Come") was Luther's translation of a hymn by Ambrose of Milan.

 "A Mighty Fortress is Our God"

Michael Praetorius (1571 – 1621) served as *kapellmeister* (person in charge of music) at Dresden and Magdeburg. He composed music for both choral and congregational singing, sometimes in interesting combinations. In many of his settings, the choir, accompanied by an instrumental ensemble, would sing an elaborate arrangement of one verse, followed by the congregation singing the next verse in unison. Similar interactions were produced by using two to four choirs singing from different parts of the church. This polychoral technique, recently developed in Vienna, created an interesting stereophonic sound. Praetorius also wrote a multi-volume encyclopaedia of music history called *Syntagma musicum.*

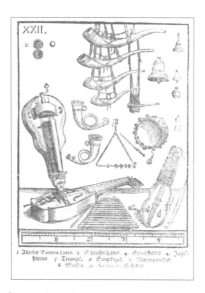

An illustration of several musical instruments from *Syntagma musicum.*

The "Pietist" movement grew out of the Lutheran Reformation. Led by Philipp Jacob Spener (1635 – 1705), the Pietists emphasised personal transformation through spiritual rebirth and renewal. They rejected some of the Lutheran liturgical ceremony, opting for a simpler form of worship. Pietist composers often paraphrased Biblical stories, psalms and canticles in order to instruct the people. The Pietist *Halle Hymnal*, published in 1741, contained 1,581 hymns and 597 tunes.

Martin Rinkart (1586 – 1649) wrote the lyrics to *Nun danket alle Gott* ("Now Thank We All Our God") from the apocryphal book of Ecclesiasticus. This famous piece was written as a hymn of thanksgiving for deliverance from the Thirty Years War and a terrible plague of 1637. It was set to music by Johann Crüger, and translated into English, in the nineteenth century, by Catherine Winkworth. Winkworth did much to introduce German hymnody to English audiences. Two other famous hymns that she translated into English are "Praise to the Lord, the Almighty" by Joachim Neander, and "All My Heart this Night Rejoices" by Paul Gerhardt.

"Now Thank We All Our God"
"Praise to the Lord, the Almighty"

Paul Gerhardt.

Paul Gerhardt (1607 – 1676) served first as probst (provost) of the Lutheran church at Mittenwald. In 1657 he was called to be a deacon of the St. Nicholas' Church in Berlin, where he became caught up in the conflict between Reformed and Lutheran clergy. This eventually led to his resignation in 1666.[30] He then ministered as archdeacon at Lübben until his death. Known as Germany's greatest hymn writer, Gerhardt wrote 133 hymns, including "O Lord, How Shall

---

[30] Phillip Jacob Spener ministered in this church from 1691 until his death in 1705.

I Meet Thee?" and "Jesus, Thy Boundless Love to Me," which was translated into English by John Wesley.

Two other famous hymns written by German hymn writers are "Jesus Lives! Thy Terrors Now . . ." by Christian Furchtegott Gellert (1715 – 1769), translated into English by Frances E. Cox, and "We Plough the Fields and Scatter," written for harvest festival by Matthias Claudius (1740 – 1815), and translated by Jane M. Campbell.

"Jesus Lives! Thy Terrors Now . . ."
"We Plough the Fields and Scatter"

The Baroque Era

During the seventeenth century, the Roman Catholic Church reformed itself and began a vigorous push to reclaim ground lost during the Reformation. This became known as the Counter-Reformation. Part of the Counter-Reformation involved a missionary thrust to take the Roman Catholic faith into the newly-explored lands of Asia and the Pacific. Part of it involved a new approach to music, which characterised the Baroque Era (1600-1750).

One of the major philosophical bases of baroque music was the belief, founded upon ancient Greek and Roman thought, that music was a powerful tool for the communication of ideas, and the stirring of emotions.

New forms of music that grew out of the Baroque Era included operas, oratorios, cantatas, concertos and sonatas.

The oratorio was "an extended musical drama with a text based on religious subject matter, intended for performance without scenery, costume or action."[31] It began in the early 1600s, with Italian composers such as Alessandro Scarlatti and Antonio Vivaldi. Later composers included Henry Purcell, J. S. Bach and Georg Frideric Handel. Small oratorios gradually became known as cantatas.

---

31   "What is Baroque Music?" *Music of the Baroque,* <https://www.baroque.org/baroque/ whatis>.

Oratorios typically included an overture, a number of arias by solo vocalists, recitative to carry forward the narrative, and some grand choruses, usually designed to signify glory.

Composers usually earned their money by writing music for a church or for a noble family. This naturally imposed some limitations on what they wrote. J. S. Bach, for example, wrote 300 cantatas, not because he particularly liked the genre, but because it was a requirement of the Leipzig church that employed him.

Composers have continued to write oratorios and cantatas right up to the present day, although many now have secular themes.

Johann Sebastian Bach (1685 – 1750)

Johann Sebastian Bach was born in the city of Eisenach, in Germany. The city was overlooked by Wartburg Castle, where Martin Luther had translated the New Testament into German 150 years previously. Bach was the outstanding member of possibly the world's greatest musical family. His talent merged with his deep Lutheran faith in God to produce some of the greatest music of all time.

Although he was a skilled violin and viola player, his main love was the organ, and it was for this instrument that he wrote many famous pieces. In 1705, he walked for 200 kilometres to spend time with the organist Dietrich Buxtehude.

In 1707, he married his second cousin Maria. She died in 1720, and the following year he married the soprano, Anna Magdalena Wilcken. Between them, the two women bore 20 children, although ten died in infancy. In 1723, Bach and his family moved to Leipzig, where he spent the rest of his life.

Although he was not entirely happy in Leipzig, he did write some of his greatest works here, including the epic *Mass in B Minor,* and the *St. Matthew Passion* and *St. John Passion.* Many of his compositions bore the inscriptions "With the help of Jesus" or "To God alone be the glory."

When Bach died in 1750, completely blind, his music was largely forgotten. Although it was resurrected by Felix Mendelssohn, who staged a performance of *St. Matthew Passion* in 1829, Bach's music has probably achieved its greatest acclamation in our own age.

Georg Frideric Handel (1685 – 1759)

Georg Frideric Handel

Unlike Bach, Georg Frideric Handel was an international celebrity. Although they lived at the same time, the two men never met.

Handel began writing music at the age of 11. From then until his death at the age of 74, he composed 42 operas, 29 oratorios and numerous other pieces of music. He lived in Germany and Italy, and then moved to Britain in 1712, where he spent the rest of his life. One of his most famous works, *Zadok the Priest*, was an anthem composed for the coronation of King George II. It has been sung at every subsequent British coronation.

A larger than life figure, Handel managed to triumph over bankruptcies, depression, the attacks of critics and eventual blindness. When the English oratorio *Esther* was first performed, in 1732, it was savagely criticised by churchmen who did not think that the theatre was a fit place for speaking the Word of God. Nevertheless, the royal family attended and the performance was a great success.

In 1741, Handel's Anglican friend, Charles Jennens, asked the composer if he could write the music for a libretto about the life of Christ and the work of redemption, with the text completely taken from the Bible. At the same time, a group of Dublin charities asked Handel if he could compose a work for a benefit performance.

On August 22, Handel started work on *Messiah*. He wrote 260 pages of music in 24 days, often going without food. When he finished writing "The Hallelujah Chorus," he confessed "I did think I did see all Heaven before me, and the great God himself." *Messiah* premiered to a sell-out crowd on April 13, 1742, at the Fishamble Street Musick Hall.

It was almost a year before *Messiah* came to London. The controversy surrounding the performance was so great that Handel renamed it "A New Sacred

Oratorio." It is said that King George II stood during "The Hallelujah Chorus," starting a tradition that has lasted until the present day. However, there does not seem to be any evidence that the king was even in attendance.

Handel died on the day before Easter 1759, hoping to "meet his good God, his sweet Lord and Savior, on the day of his Resurrection." One book, assessing the life of Handel, comments, "Much modern music batters the listener and adds to the noise and confusion in our already noisy and confusing lives. The music of Handel helps to bring order and joy into living."[32]

Messiah is performed annually, so try and attend a live performance. Alternatively, listen to an audio recording or watch a video clip.

Other famous pieces from oratorios include:

"Oh Sacred Head" from *St. Matthew Passion* by J. S. Bach. This is based on a poem attributed to the Medieval abbot Arnulf of Leuven (died 1250) and translated into German by Paul Gerhardt.

"Arrival of the Queen of Sheba" from *Solomon* by Handel

"Let There Be Light" or "The Heavens are Telling the Glory of God" from *The Creation* by Joseph Haydn

"If with All Your Hearts" from *Elijah* by Felix Mendelssohn

"God So Loved the World" from *The Crucifixion* by John Stainer

---

[32]   Jane Stuart Smith and Betty Carlson, *The Gift of Music: Great Composers and Their Influence*, Crossway Books, Wheaton, 1995, p. 46.

CHAPTER SIX

CALVIN, WATTS AND WESLEY

John Calvin (1509 – 1564)

While Luther was warm and outgoing, with a love for life and music, Calvin was "cold, and ordered, lacking a sense of humor or a noticeable appreciation for beauty in life or art."[33] Ultimately, however, it was Calvin who had more influence than Luther. Luther was basically a German nationalist, and his influence was primarily tied to that one country. Calvin, on the other hand, was not a nationalist, and Calvinism had a wide influence all over the world.

John Calvin

John Calvin was a brilliant student. As a young man, he entered the field of law and studied at different universities, including Paris. When he was about 24 years of age, he was converted, probably as a result of reading Luther's works. He left France and settled in Switzerland. Three years later, he published one of the greatest books ever written. It was called *Institutes of the Christian Religion*. His writings attracted the attention of the reformer, William Farel. Farel invited him to come to the city of Geneva, and it was here that Calvin was to live for the rest of his life (apart for a three-year period when he was exiled from there).

---

[33] Cusic, *op. cit.*, p. 20.

As well as pastoring St. Pierre Church, Calvin wrote dozens of pamphlets, and commentaries on almost every book in the Bible. Despite various illnesses, including migraine headaches, he corresponded with many people and trained scores of missionaries.

Calvin wanted Geneva to be like the kingdom of God on earth. Although he met with much opposition, he was eventually able to reform the whole city with the support of the city council. The Scotsman, John Knox (founder of the Presbyterian Church), described Geneva as "the most perfect school of Christ since the days of the apostles."

Calvin established four types of ministry:

- Doctors were scholars who taught the people and trained other ministers.
- Pastors looked after the spiritual welfare of the people. They preached the Gospel and administered the sacraments.
- Deacons were laymen who provided for the physical welfare of the people. They looked after hospitals and anti-poverty programmes.
- Elders were 12 laymen whose task was to serve as a kind of moral police force. They could warn people who were misbehaving, but if the problem continued they could refer them to the Consistory.

The Consistory was a court made up of pastors and elders. Its job was to keep order amongst the people of the city. Wild singing, for example, might be punished by tongue piercing. If you worked on Sunday, you might be required to attend some public sermons or catechism classes. For really bad sins, you might be excommunicated (that is, cast out of the church). Then you would have to leave Geneva. Although this might sound rather strict to us, we must remember that Calvin was keen to promote the health and well-being of individuals, families and communities. Recently discovered documents show that the Consistory was very concerned about home life and protecting women.

Calvin was also concerned about education. He realised that if his ideas were to be spread throughout Europe, he would need to train up men for the job. So he created primary and secondary schools, and in 1559 the Academy was created that would become the University of Geneva. By 1564 there were over 1,500 university students, and most of these were from other countries.

Calvin died in 1564, but his teachings found a home in places as far apart as Scotland, Poland, Holland, and America. They are still the foundation of the Reformed and Presbyterian churches world-wide.

The Church of England

From the publication of the vernacular *Book of Common Prayer* in 1549, through to the English Civil War of the 1640s, (with the exception of a brief period, from 1553 to 1558, when Queen Mary I sought to reintroduce Catholicism), a simplified form of the Mass was used in the Anglican churches of Britain. Although Queen Elizabeth I sanctioned the singing of some hymns, the increasing influence of the Calvinistic Puritans in the Church largely ruled out the use of musical instruments and choirs. One form of music that became associated with the Anglican liturgy was the anthem.

 Listen to the anthem "Hosanna to the Son of David" by Orlando Gibbons

Psalm singing remained very popular, and a metrical psalter called *The Whole Book of Psalms* was published by Thomas Sternhold and John Hopkins in 1562, and expanded by Thomas Ravenscroft in 1621. This contained tunes – such as WINCHESTER OLD, DURHAM and CHESHIRE - that are still used in churches today. This "Old Version," as it was called, was often criticized for the poor quality of its lyrics. *A New Version of the Psalms of David* was published by Nahum Tate and Nicholas Brady in 1696. "Hymns" that first made their appearance in this book include "While Shepherds watched Their Flocks by Night" and "Through All the Changing Scenes of Life."

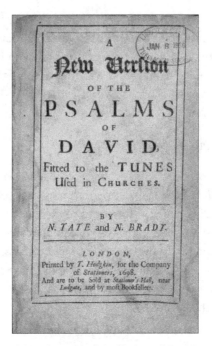

A New Version of the Psalms of David.

 "Through All the Changing Scenes of Life"

From 1645 to 1660, during the time of the English Republic, *The Book of Common Prayer*, musical instruments, and all forms of church music except metrical psalm singing were banned. With the restoration of King Charles II, however, there was a rebirth of musical innovation. The king even introduced violins to the Chapel Royal – a very daring move, and one that occasioned some criticism.

The 1662 revision of *The Book of Common Prayer* contained the famous quotation "In quires and places where they sing, here followeth the anthem." Famous anthem writers included Henry Purcell, William Boyce and William Croft. Croft wrote the tune ST. ANNE, to which Isaac Watts later set the words "Oh God Our Help."

Isaac Watts (1674 – 1748)

Isaac Watts was a Calvinist. He grew up in a Non-Conformist household where his father, like his contemporary John Bunyan, spent time in prison for refusing to embrace the established Church of England.

Isaac Watts

Although of sickly constitution, Watts had a brilliant mind and had mastered several languages, including Greek and Hebrew, during his childhood and early teenage years. His love of rhyme sometimes exasperated his father. While receiving corporal correction for having his eyes open during family prayers, he is reported to have cried out "O father, father, pity take, And I will no more verses make."

Unable to attend Oxford or Cambridge Universities because of his Non-Conformist sympathies, he studied at the Dissenting Academy in Stoke Newington. In 1702, he became pastor of Mark Lane Independent Chapel, but had to resign ten years later due to mental health issues.

This illness, plus his unprepossessing appearance are probably the reasons why he never married. Taken in by the wealthy Abney family, he spent the rest of his life in their household.

His first collection of hymns - *Hymns and Spiritual Songs* – was published in 1707. His scholarship went far beyond hymn-writing, however. He published many other works on a variety of subjects, including an influential textbook on Logic. He also wrote a book of children's verse.

Against Idleness and Mischief

How doth the little busy Bee
Improve each shining Hour,
And gather Honey all the day
From every opening Flower!

How skilfully she builds her Cell!
How neat she spreads the Wax!
And labours hard to store it well
With the sweet Food she makes.
In Works of Labour or of Skill
I would be busy too:
For Satan finds some Mischief still
For idle Hands to do.
In Books, or Work, or healthful Play
Let my first Years be past,
That I may give for every Day
Some good Account at last.

Calvin's theology was based on the concept of the absolute sovereignty of God. God is an absolute ruler in total control of everything. Therefore nothing happens without God willing it to happen. Everything that has ever happened has been in accordance with His will.

This leads on to the doctrine of strict predestination. Humans have no choice in their eternal destiny. They are either destined to be saved or not to be saved before they are born. "In the tragedy of human history, Christ is a figure of redemption only for the privileged few chosen for heaven even before their birth."[34]

This naturally impacted the music that Calvinist songwriters composed. Calvin himself encouraged congregational singing, but whereas hymns continued to be sung in Lutheran churches, only the Psalms were to be sung in Calvinist assemblies, and no musical instruments were to be used. Eventually all the Psalms were put to music in the *Genevan Psalter*.

Although he was a Calvinist, Isaac Watts broke away from Calvinism in one respect. From a young age, he was concerned about the standard of congregational singing. "To see the dull indifference, the negligent and thoughtless air

---

[34]   *Ibid.*, p. 46.

that sits upon the faces of a whole assembly, while the psalm is upon their lips, might even tempt a charitable observer to suspect the fervency of their inward religion."

Watt put forward the theory that "religious songs are a human offering of praise to God, and therefore the words should be personal."[35] Naturally, he had to face considerable opposition before his ideas were accepted in the church.

In his song "We're Marching to Zion," Watt replies to his opponents who had branded his hymns as "Watts' Whims."

> The sorrows of the mind
> Be banished from the place;
> Religion never was designed
> To make our pleasures less.
>
> Let those refuse to sing,
> Who never knew our God;
> But favorites of the heavenly King
> May speak their joys abroad.

Watts also believed that the Psalms needed to be rewritten, in song, to reflect both the Christian message and British nationalism. His hymn "Before Jehovah's Awful Throne," for example, was based on Psalm 100. The first verse reads:

> Sing to the Lord with joyful voice;
> Let every land his name adore;
> The British Isles shall send the noise
> Across the ocean to the shore.

This verse was subsequently edited out by the Wesleys before they published the hymn.

---

[35] *Ibid.*, p. 45

The songs that Watt wrote were simple in meter and sung to whatever popular tune was chosen by the clerk of the assembly. Using a method known as "lining out," the clerk would announce a line and the congregation would sing it. It is hard for us to imagine, but it took the congregation of Watts' own church several years to master the art of hymn-singing!

Of course there was no appeal to lost souls in Watts' hymns because humans did not have the option to change – why try and save them when they cannot be saved? Evangelical outreach had to wait for the Wesleyan Revival later in the eighteenth century.

 "When I Survey the Wondrous Cross"

"Jesus Shall Reign Wher'er the Sun"

"Joy to the World" This was not originally written for Christmas, which the Non-Conformists believed to be a pagan holiday. It is sung to a tune by Georg Frideric Handel.

"Oh God Our Help"

"We're Marching to Zion"

"At the Cross"

The Wesleyan Revival

The eighteenth century was the century of revolution. Both France and the American colonies experienced violent revolutions, and it seemed likely that England would follow the same path. The country, at the beginning of the eighteenth century, was in a mess, morally and spiritually. The historian, Thomas Carlyle, described the country's condition as, "Stomach well alive, soul extinct." Sir William Blackstone, the famous judge and author, visited every major church in London, but did not hear a single sermon that exalted the Lord Jesus Christ. Gambling and drunkenness were common everywhere, newborn babies were abandoned in the streets, bear baiting and cock fighting were accepted sports, and tickets were sold to public executions as to a theatre. Four out of five children died.

Into this spiritual malaise strode George Whitefield and his two friends, John and Charles Wesley.

John Wesley (1703 – 1791)
Charles Wesley (1707 – 1778)

John Wesley was the fifteenth child of Samuel Wesley and his wife Susanna Wesley. Samuel Wesley was a poet who, from 1696, was rector of Epworth. He married Susanna, the twenty-fifth child of Samuel Annesley, a dissenting minister, in 1689. Ultimately, she bore him nineteen children, of which nine lived beyond infancy.

John Wesley.
By John Faber (1695-1756).

Susanna was instrumental in the early education of her children. Each child, including the girls, was taught to read as soon as he or she could walk and talk. They were expected to become proficient in Latin and Greek and to have learned major portions of the New Testament by heart. In 1714, at age 11, John Wesley was sent to the Charterhouse School in London. Six years later, he entered Christ Church, Oxford, where he eventually received a Master of Arts degree, while working as a fellow and tutor at the university.

Brother Charles was educated at Westminster School before entering Oxford, where he too obtained a Master's degree. While at Oxford, both John and Charles met with other students in an attempt to find salvation through self-denial and good works. Their zeal earned them the nickname of the "Holy Club." Later, the Wesley brothers went to Georgia, in America, to work as missionaries to the Indians. They returned in despair. "I went to America to convert the Indians," John wrote, "but O who will convert me!"

On the ship going to Georgia, the Wesleys had met some Moravian immigrants who had impressed them with their spiritual strength and joy in the Lord. Back in England, as the brothers struggled with their own sinfulness and need of salvation, they received spiritual counsel from the Moravian Peter Boehler. Both came to a saving faith in Christ in May 1738.

From their friend George Whitefield, they learned the importance of preaching in the open air to reach the masses. Although they tried to remain within the Church of England, their so-called "enthusiasm" soon led to closed church doors and to active persecution. They were forced to preach in the open fields, or wherever they could gather a crowd.

While John had an unhappy marriage, which eventually ended in separation, Charles married happily and had eight children, although only three survived to adulthood. Both his son Samuel (1766 – 1837) and his grandson Samuel Sebastian (1810 – 1876) wrote important music for the Roman Catholic and Anglican Churches respectively.

Ill-health forced Charles to withdraw from itinerant ministry after 1756, but John continued to travel, covering about 400,000 kilometres on horseback and preaching up to 15 sermons a week. He also supervised the education of lay preachers who could teach and disciple people in small cell groups. These preachers also distributed and sold Christian books to the people, helping provide them with spiritual food. Wesley was the first to print and use religious tracts extensively.

The Wesley's followers became known as "Methodists" because of the way they used "rule" and "method" to go about their religious affairs. By the time John and Charles died, there were about 100,000 Methodists in Britain, although both brothers remained within the Church of England, and the Methodist Church, as such, did not come into existence until after John's death, in 1791.

The revival that George Whitefield, John Wesley and his hymn writer-brother, Charles, began, transformed English society. Antislavery societies, prison reform groups, and relief agencies for the poor were started. Numerous missionary societies were formed; the Religious Tract Society was organized; and the British and Foreign Bible Society was established. Hospitals and schools multiplied. In 1928 Archbishop Davidson wrote that "Wesley practically changed the outlook and even the character of the English nation."[36]

---

[36] *The Times*, November 2, 1928.

The Wesley brothers differed from Calvin and Isaac Watts in their opposition to the doctrine of strict predestination. While acknowledging the sovereignty of God, John followed the Dutch theologian Arminius (1560-1609) in believing that Christ's death on the cross atoned for the sins of all men, not just a chosen few. John stated that predestination made "God worse than the devil." Quoting 2 Peter 3:9 - "The Lord is not willing that any should perish, but that all should come to repentance" – he argued that all men have the choice of either accepting or rejecting the salvation that God extends freely by His grace. This created some tension with George Whitefield, who remained a "Calvinistic Methodist."

In his lifetime, Charles Wesley wrote over 6,500 hymns, many of which have a clear evangelical message. One of his most famous hymns, "Oh for a Thousand Tongues," for example, contains the lines "He sets the prisoner free/His blood can make the foulest clean," which is a clear statement of the doctrine of free will. Like Isaac Watts, he also paraphrased many of the Psalms, expressing them in terms of Christian doctrine.

The first Anglican hymn book – *Collections of Psalms and Hymns* – was published in 1737. It appears that none of Charles Wesley's hymns were included, but over the next 40 years, until his death in 1778, Charles published 56 volumes of hymns and psalms. In 1780, John published *A Collection of Hymns for the Use of the People Called Methodists*. The 525 hymns in this volume were not only to be used for praise and worship, but also to teach Christian doctrine to new converts who were unfamiliar with the Bible.

In their book *The Fountain of Public Prosperity*, Stuart Piggin and Robert Linder state that "It was through the Methodists that the door was unlocked to the use of hymns in British Protestant worship, supplementing the singing of metrical psalmody and opening the way to propagating doctrine in a manner often more accessible and memorable than reading and preaching. It was not so much that Methodists won the theological debate by argument; they won it largely unnoticed by singing."[37]

---

[37]   Stuart Piggin and Robert D. Linder, *The Fountain of Public Prosperity: Evangelical Christians in Australian History, 1740 - 1914*, Monash University Publishing, Clayton, Victoria, 2018, pp. 318-319.

The Wesleys took song writing seriously – "In these hymns there is no bad verse; no poor or clumsy work; no unnecessary words. Here is no fancy language with little meaning, on one hand, or low and meaningless colloquialisms that insult the intelligence of the hearer, on the other. Here are the purity, strength and beauty of the English language; and, at the same time, the utmost simplicity and plainness, suited to every person's understanding" [*quotation paraphrased by the author*].

In terms of the volume of songs he wrote, and the quality of the lyrics, Charles Wesley deserves to be called the greatest hymn writer of all time.

 "Oh For a Thousand Tongues"
"Christ the Lord is Risen Today"
"Hark, the Herald Angels Sing" - Music by Felix Mendelssohn
"Love Divine"
"And Can It Be"

John Newton (1725 – 1807)

John Newton was the son of a commander of a merchant ship that sailed the Mediterranean. As a young man, he was impressed (kidnapped) into service in the Royal Navy. Conditions on board *HMS Harwich* were so bad that he deserted, only to be recaptured, flogged, and demoted from midshipman to common seaman.

At his own request, he was exchanged into service on a slave ship, which took him to the coast of

John Newton

Sierra Leone, where he became the servant of a slave dealer and was brutally abused. Early in 1748, he was rescued by a sea captain who had known John's father.

On the way back to England, the ship encountered a fierce storm, and was in danger of sinking. In despair, he cried out to God and experienced what he considered to be a moment of conversion. As he himself admitted, however, ""I cannot consider myself to have been a believer in the full sense of the word, until a considerable time afterwards."

Back in England he began to study the Bible and other Christian literature. He also married his sweetheart of many years, Mary Catlett, in 1750. However, he continued in the slave trade, eventually becoming the captain of his own slave ship.

In 1755, after a serious illness, he left the sea and became surveyor of tides in Liverpool. During these years, he came to know both George Whitefield and John Wesley. He was ordained to the Anglican ministry in 1764 and took the parish of Olney, in Buckinghamshire. In 1880, he left here to become rector at St. Mary Woolnoth, in London.

In his later years, Newton strongly supported the anti-slavery lobby, and encouraged William Wilberforce in his crusade. A law was passed banning the African slave trade in 1807, the year of Newton's death.

John Newton is primarily remembered for his hymn "Amazing Grace" (originally called "Faith's Review and Expectation"). This hymn would have originally been chanted, and then sung to a variety of different tunes. Newton died before the tune we use today – NEW BRITAIN - was paired with the lyrics. The origin of NEW BRITAIN is unknown (it may have originated as a folk song), but the first printed version of this tune and the lyrics was made in 1835 by American singing master William Walker, in his shaped-note tune book *Southern Harmony.*

"Amazing Grace" as it appeared in the 1847 edition of *Southern Harmony*.

The verse beginning "When we've been there ten thousand years" was not written by John Newton. It appears to have been passed down orally in African American communities and made an appearance in Harriet Beecher Stowe's influential 1852 anti-slavery novel *Uncle Tom's Cabin*. Later, it was included in various church hymnals.

Newton wrote many other hymns, often in collaboration with the poet, William Cowper, who was a member of his congregation in Olney. The two men tried to write a new song for each weekly prayer meeting, and they published several editions of hymns, under the title *Olney Hymns*.

 "Amazing Grace"

"Glorious Things of Thee Are Spoken" - Music by Haydn

"How Sweet the Name of Jesus Sounds"

Hymns Ancient and Modern

Hymn-singing was officially frowned upon in the Anglican Church until the 1820s. To the establishment, hymns "represented 'enthusiasm', emotionalism, and sectarianism – everything they despised in the practice of religion."[38]

When Thomas Cotterill, curate of St. Paul's Church, Sheffield, received permission from the archbishop to use hymns in his church, however, the floodgates were opened. In the following years, thousands of hymns were written or translated by men such as James Montgomery ("Angels from the Realms of Glory"), Reginald Heber ("Holy, Holy, Holy, Lord God Almighty"), William Walsham How ("For all the Saints"), John Mason Neale ("Good Christian Men, Rejoice"), Henry Francis Lyte ("Praise, My Soul, the King of Heaven" and "Abide with Me"), William Whiting ("Eternal Father, Strong to Save"), and John Ellerton ("The Day Thou Gavest, Lord, Is Ended").

New tunes were also written by men such as John Dykes, John Stainer, John Goss and William Henry Monk. Sir Arthur Sullivan (of Gilbert and Sullivan fame) wrote the march ST. GERTRUDE for Sabine Baring-Gould's popular hymn "Onward Christian Soldiers."

In 1861, the first Anglican hymnal was created. Called *Hymns Ancient and Modern,* it contained hymns from a variety of sources, both within the Church and from outside. Some of the hymns by Watts and the Wesley brothers were included. The hymnal was amazingly successful, selling four and a half million copies in the first seven years. It was the first hymnbook to include the tune on the same page as the lyrics, and it has continued to the present day. The 2000 edition had the title *Common Praise.*

---

[38] Dowley, *op. cit.,* p. 166.

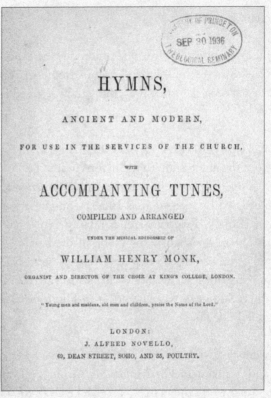

Title page of the first edition of *Hymns Ancient and Modern.*

"Abide with Me" – Listen to this song which, amongst other things, is traditionally sung at the FA Cup Final at Wembley Stadium, London.

"Eternal Father, Strong to Save" is the official "Navy Hymn."
"Onward Christian Soldiers"

You may listen to other hymns mentioned above.

CHAPTER SEVEN

GREAT AWAKENINGS IN AMERICA

It seems that the first church songs sung in North America were Gregorian chants associated with the Spanish Catholic churches of the southern parts of the continent.

The Puritans, who settled in New England, came from the Calvinist tradition. They sang only Psalms and used no musical instruments. The two Psalters most widely used were the *Bay Psalm Book* (1640) and Sternhold and Hopkins's *Whole Book of Psalms* (the "Old Version," 1562). The Psalms were usually sung slowly and reverently, but because they were sung from word books only, congregational singing was very bad, as everyone sang his or her own version.

One solution was the singing school, with its singing master, where people were trained to read music and to sing the proper tunes for Psalms. "The singing master generally canvassed the neighbourhood, assembled a class, and engaged a large room which might be a schoolhouse, a church, or a tavern. He taught the rudiments of notation, a method of beating time, and solemnization. These principles were applied to psalm tunes, and the session terminated with an 'exhibition' in which the class sang the tunes which they had learned to their assembled relatives, friends, and neighbours."[39] The printing of books with both words and melody also helped.

---

[39] This is quoted in Cusic, *op. cit.*, p. 37. It is attributed to Charles Hughes, *American Hymns Old and New*, but this appears to be an incorrect reference.

There was a negative effect of singing schools and printed tune books, however. In the Catholic, Lutheran and Anglican Church traditions, singing shifted from congregations to choirs. Rather than being a living and vital part of congregational worship, it became accepted as an art form.

First Great Awakening

A defining event in the history of Christian music in America was the First Great Awakening of the 1700s (1730 - 1755). This was an extension of the Wesleyan Revival which was impacting Britain at the time. The two men most closely associated with this Awakening were Jonathan Edwards and George Whitefield.

Jonathan Edwards (1703 - 1758)

Jonathan Edwards was a Reformed Congregational pastor, theologian and missionary. His father was a pastor, and Jonathan was the only boy amongst ten sisters, all six feet tall! He entered Yale University at age 12, and graduated with a Bachelor of Arts degree in 1720 and a Master of Arts degree in 1722. During his final year at college, he gained an assurance of salvation, which set the course of his life.

Jonathan Edwards

After a short period working as a supply preacher at a Presbyterian Church in New York, Edwards tutored at Yale for two years. In 1726, however, he was appointed as assistant pastor to his grandfather's church in Northampton, in New England. He remained there for 23 years, during which time he married his teenage sweetheart, Sarah Pierpont, who produced 11 children.

After the death of his grandfather, Edwards became concerned that many of the members of his congregation were only nominal Christians. This was somewhat alleviated by a local revival that broke out in 1734-35, and became part of the Great Awakening that swept the eastern seaboard. Edwards became an eager participant in the Awakening. His most famous sermon was called *Sinners in the Hands of an Angry God*. In truth, however, Edwards did not shout or speak loudly, and he frequently preached on the great love of God.

There was some controversy over bodily manifestations of the Holy Spirit that accompanied the Awakening. Today, these things are common in many Pentecostal circles, but in the more conservative Reformed churches of New England, such expressions were often regarded as, at the best, mere hysterical outbursts. Edwards was forced to defend these supernatural evidences of the Holy Spirit, partly because he witnessed them close at hand, in his own wife, Sarah.

More serious trouble arose over the Lord's Supper. Edwards came to the conclusion that Communion should only be taken by those who demonstrated unmistakeable evidence of Christian conversion. His opponents eventually forced him out of the church.

He and his family moved to the small settlement of Stockbridge, Massachusetts, where his pastoral duties also involved missionary outreach to the local Indian population. Edwards also used his time here to write many of the theological and philosophical works that today fill up over 27 thick volumes.

The final chapter of his life occupied less than a year. In 1757, he was unexpectedly called to be president of Princeton University. After his arrival there, in 1758, he was faced with an outbreak of smallpox. Being a keen supporter of science, he agreed to try a new smallpox vaccination. Sadly, the vaccination caused his death, at the age of 54.

His colonial followers distinguished themselves from other Congregationalists as "New Lights" (endorsing the Great Awakening), as opposed to "Old Lights" (non-revivalists).

George Whitefield (1714 - 1770)

George Whitefield

George Whitefield was a friend of the Wesley brothers, and instrumental in the formation of Methodism. While at Oxford University, he joined the "Holy Club." Later, he decided, like the Wesleys, to do mission work in the new American colony of Georgia. While waiting for a passage, he was ordained as a deacon in the Anglican Church and preached around London.

His preaching methods were very unconventional. He had always been interested in acting, and although he repudiated the theatre, he used many of its methods. He would cry, or dance, or scream, as he portrayed various Biblical characters. His small stature and cross-eyed appearance added to the interest. Crowds flocked to hear him.

Whitefield eventually made it to Georgia, but he only stayed there a short time. He did, however, found an orphanage that consumed much of his money for the rest of his life.

Back in England, he found, like the Wesleys, that many churches were closing their doors to him. So he began experimenting with outdoor preaching.

In 1739, he undertook a preaching tour of the American colonies, the second of seven visits to North America. His popularity preceded him, aided, no doubt, by his judicious use of the printing press to advertise his visits. He would sometimes preach to audiences of over 20,000, and remember that this was long before the use of modern sound systems! His meetings became part of the Great Awakening, and it is estimated that virtually every man, woman and child in the colonies would have heard him preach at least once.

Whitefield was not afraid of controversy. His meetings were sometimes broken up by unruly mobs, and he himself was physically attacked several times. He was fearless in his condemnation of traditional churches that preached only the "shell and shadow" of Christianity.

Just before his death at the age of 55, Whitefield said, "I would rather wear out than rust out." A biographer has stated that "George Whitefield was probably the most famous religious figure of the eighteenth century. Newspapers called him the 'marvel of the age'. Whitefield was a preacher capable of commanding thousands on two continents through the sheer power of his oratory. In his lifetime, he preached at least 18,000 times to perhaps 10 million hearers."[40]

Transition

As in Britain, the transition from psalms to hymns was long and difficult. The First Great Awakening provided the spark that brought an influx of new songs into the church. It began with Isaac Watts, and progressed through the Wesleyan Methodists. Both Jonathan Edwards and George Whitefield used Watts' hymns. The lively tunes and catchy lyrics accorded well with Whitefield's style of preaching. Between 1738 and 1743, six reprints of Watts' hymns appeared from American presses. The Wesleys' *Hymns and Sacred Poems* was reprinted in Philadelphia in 1740.

There was a similar scenario with the use of musical instruments. It was not until 1792 that the clarinet and the violin were first played in church in Massachusetts. The introduction of the base viol (short-necked cello) caused violent opposition. The organ gradually came to be accepted as the proper instrument for congregational worship, however, the Scottish Presbyterians were the last to give in regarding the use of instruments and hymns.

The First Great Awakening greatly impacted the African-American people. Both Edwards and Whitefield were slave owners, but they did not exclude slaves from their meetings. Preachers often believed that it was in the interests of the slave owners to educate their slaves so that they could read the Bible. Many African-Americans were converted to Christianity at this time, and a number of black churches were established. Some historians see the First Great Awakening as the birthplace of African-American Christianity.

---

40   "George Whitefield: Sensational Evangelist of Britain and America," <http://www.christianitytoday.com/history/people/evangelistsandapologists/george-whitefield.html>

Second Great Awakening

Between the years 1775 and 1777, the American colonists fought a War of Independence with Britain. A number of sacred songs were associated with this war, usually of a patriotic nature. William Billings (1746 – 1800) was a singing master who wrote what became known as the "Battle Hymn of the Revolution." The song, "Let Tyrants Shake Their Iron Rods," was set to the tune CHESTER. It was sung in home, schools and churches, and was also a popular marching song used by the colonists as they went into battle. The "slavery" referred to in the following stanza was not the slavery of the African-Americans, but rather the colonists' supposed "slavery" to the British "tyrants."

> Let tyrants shake their iron rods,
> And slavery clank her galling chains:
> We see them not; we trust in God:
> New England's God forever reigns.

CHESTER – "Let Tyrants Shake Their Iron Rods"

After the war, another revival broke out between 1780 and 1830. This has become known as the Second Great Awakening.

Whereas the First Great Awakening had mainly impacted the Reformed churches of the New England region, the Second Great Awakening was associated more with frontier preachers of Baptist, Methodist (Arminian) and Presbyterian persuasion.

As the country pushed westwards, revival fires sprang up here and there. These were not initially organised along denominational lines. Indeed, the people involved usually lived beyond the influence of the established churches. Revival preachers spoke to the common, rural, farming communities wherever they could get an audience.

"Camp meetings" were the norm. These were held in frontier areas, where people without regular preachers would travel, often long distances, to a particular site. Here they would camp out for a few days, listen to a variety of itinerant preachers, pray and sing hymns. Often there would be manifestations of the Holy Spirit, or of extreme emotion, including speaking in tongues, falling over (what would today be called being "slain in the Spirit"), jerking the head rapidly, rolling on the ground, and dancing, sometimes for hours at a time. Camp meetings offered not only spiritual comfort, but also social interaction, and a diversion from the rigors of work.

A camp meeting c. 1829.

This was folk religion. The rich and the urban areas back east were rejected as sinful. Every individual had direct access to God. "The religious awakening of the settlers put the principle of voluntarism (churches being supported freely by members) before liturgy, democracy before orthodoxy, and emotionalism before an intellectual, rational approach to religion. Denominational lines were broken and crossed as the church reached the masses . . . revivalism stressed the work of man in salvation as well as the sovereignty of God."[41]

The songs that were sung were often based on folk tunes – sometimes secular songs with Christian words – but they could also be made up on the spot, using a Scripture verse, or a line from a preacher's sermon, as a starting point.

---

[41]   Cusic, *op. cit.*, p. 103

These were simple songs, with a lot of repetition, so that they could be easily learned by the members of the congregation. Sometimes the repetition would be in the form of verse and chorus. The song leader would sing the verses and the audience would respond with the chorus.

Lift up your hearts, Immanuel's friends,
And taste the pleasure Jesus sends;
Let nothing cause you to delay,
But hasten on the good old way.

Chorus:
And I'll sing hallelujah,
And glory to God on high;
And I'll sing hallelujah,
There's glory beaming through the sky.
Camp-Meeting Chorister, No. 105

At other times repetition would be in the form of call-and-response. The song leader would sing a line in the form of a statement or question, and the audience would respond with the next line.

I've 'listed in the holy war,
Sing glory, glory, hallelujah.
Content to suffer soldiers' fare;
Sing glory, glory, hallelujah.
The banner over me is love,
Sing glory, glory, hallelujah.
I draw my rations from above.
Sing glory, glory, hallelujah.
Camp-Meeting Chorister, No. 114

Collections of camp meeting hymns were published in volumes such as *The Pilgrims' Songster* (1828) and *The Camp-Meeting Chorister* (1830).

The Kentucky Revival of 1800 was typical of the Second Great Awakening. It impacted not only the state of Kentucky, but also parts of Tennessee and southern Ohio. A Presbyterian minister, Barton W. Stone, recorded his impressions of an early camp meeting.

Many, very many, fell down as men slain in battle, and continued for hours together in an apparently breathless and motionless state, sometimes for a few moments reviving and exhibiting symptoms of life by a deep groan or piercing shriek, or by a prayer for mercy fervently uttered. After lying there for hours they obtained deliverance. The gloomy cloud that had covered their faces seemed gradually and visibly to disappear, and hope, in smiles, brightened into joy. They would rise, shouting deliverance, and then would address the surrounding multitude in language truly eloquent and impressive. With astonishment did I hear men, women, and children declaring the wonderful works of God and the glorious mysteries of the gospel.

Stone went on to minister at the Cane Ridge Revival of 1801, which was attended by an estimated 20,000 people.

"Sinners dropping down on every hand, shrieking, groaning, crying for mercy, convoluted," one witness said, "professors [believers] praying, agonizing, fainting, falling down in distress for sinners, or in raptures of joy! Some singing, some shouting, clapping their hands, hugging and even kissing, laughing; others talking to the distressed, to one another, or to opposers of the work, and all this at once."

One person who was converted during the Kentucky Revival was Peter Cartwright. As a teenager, Cartwright spent months agonizing over his sinful condition. Eventually he attended a camp meeting.

On the Saturday evening of said meeting, I went, with weeping multitudes, and bowed before the stand, and earnestly prayed for mercy. In the midst of a solemn struggle of soul, an impression was made on my mind, as though a voice said to me, "Thy sins are all forgiven thee." Divine light flashed all round me, unspeakable joy sprung up in my soul. I rose to my feet, opened my eyes, and it really seemed as if I was in heaven; the trees, the leaves on them, and everything seemed, and I really thought were, praising God. My mother raised the shout, my Christian friends crowded around me and joined me in praising God; and though I have been since then, in many instances, unfaithful, yet I have never, for one moment, doubted that the Lord did, then and there, forgive my sins and give me religion.

Peter Cartwright

Cartwright went on to become a Methodist circuit rider, and, eventually, a member of the Illinois legislature. He was a charismatic preacher, and it is estimated that he personally baptised about 12,000 converts.

One of the songs that became associated with Cartwright's ministry was "Where Are the Hebrew Children?" The origin of this song is unclear but it is typical of the songs that were associated with camp meetings. There is lots of repetition and room for improvisation. The song is based on the story of the three Israelites in the fiery furnace (Daniel 3:21). Subsequent verses go on to ask the whereabouts of various Bible characters and of "holy Christians." The answer is always the same – "Safe in the Promised Land."

 "Where Are the Hebrew Children?"

Another song commonly sung was "I Am a Poor Wayfaring Stranger." This tells the story of a Christian's journey through life.

I am a poor wayfaring stranger
A-trav'ling through this land of woe.
And there's no sickness, toil or danger

In that bright world to which I go.

I'm going home to see my father.
I'm going there no more to roam;
I'm just a-going over Jordan
I'm just a-going over home.

The Second Great Awakening gave rise to a number of new denominations. These included the Stone-Campbell Restoration Movement that sought the unification of all Christians into one body. The Churches of Christ trace their origins to this movement. Also significant were the various Adventist churches that looked to the imminent Second Coming of Jesus. These began with the followers of William Miller (hence the name Millerites) and culminated in the formation of the Seventh Day Adventist Church.

 "Wayfaring Stranger"

Negro spirituals

The genre of religious songs known as "Negro Spirituals" is unique to the African-American experience in the United States. As black Americans became exposed to the teachings of Christianity at camp meetings, they adapted what they heard to suit their condition.

> My people told stories from Genesis to Revelation, with God's faithful as the main characters. They knew about Adam and Eve in the Garden, about Moses and the Red Sea. They sang of the Hebrew children and Joshua at the battle of Jericho. They could tell you about Mary, Jesus, God, and the Devil. If you stood around long enough, you'd hear a song about the blind man seeing, God troubling the water, Ezekiel seeing a wheel, Jesus being crucified and raised from the dead. If slaves couldn't read the Bible, they could memorize Biblical stories they heard and translate them into songs.[42]

---

[42] Velma Maia Thomas, *No Man Can Hinder Me: The Journey from Slavery to Emancipation through Song*, Crown Publishers, New York, 2001, p. 14.

Naturally, many of the spirituals related to the condition of slavery. The Israelites' exodus from slavery in Egypt was a popular theme.

Let My People Go

When Israel was in Egypt's land:
Let my people go,
Oppress'd so hard they could not stand,
Let my People go.

Chorus:
Go down, Moses,
Way down in Egypt's land,
Tell old Pharaoh,
Let my people go.

In the song "Israel" represents the African-American slaves while "Egypt" and "Pharaoh" represent the slave master.

Another theme dealt with the crossing of Jordan River, which signified death and release from physical bondage. It could also refer to escaping to the northern states or to Canada on the underground railway.

Swing Low, Sweet Chariot

Swing low, sweet chariot
Coming for to carry me home,
Swing low, sweet chariot,
Coming for to carry me home.

I looked over Jordan, and what did I see?
Coming for to carry me home.
I saw a band of angels coming after me,
Coming for to carry me home.

Deep River

Deep River,
My home is over Jordan.
Deep River, Lord.
I want to cross over into campground.

The first compilation of Negro Spirituals was *Slave Songs of the United States*, published in 1867. The editor commented on the difficulty of transcribing "the intonations and delicate variations of even one singer" on to paper.

A song from the 1867 compilation *Slave Songs of the United States*.

The song "Give Me That Old Time Religion" is of unknown origin. Charles Davis Tillman heard it being sung by a group of African-Americans in 1889, and appropriated it for white southern churches. It thus became a formative influence in the genre known as Southern Gospel, and was used in the famous World War One movie *Sergeant York*.

Another song whose origin is unknown is "Just a Closer Walk with Thee." It is thought that the song may have come out of the African-American churches of the 1800s – possibly even before the American Civil War of the 1860s. The first known recording was by the Selah Jubilee Singers in 1941.

Thus both Black Gospel and Southern Gospel grew out of the spiritual ferment of the Second Great Awakening.

 Listen to, or sing, some of the following Spirituals.

"Let My People Go"

"Swing Low, Sweet Chariot"

"Deep River"

"Were You There?"

(the first spiritual to be included in a modern hymn book, in 1940)

"Every Time I Feel the Spirit"

"Standin' in the Need of Prayer"

"Nobody Knows the Trouble I've Seen"

"Let Us Break Bread Together"

"I Got a Robe"

"Down by the Riverside"

"Roll Jordan, Roll"

"Give Me that Old Time Religion"

"Just a Closer Walk with Thee"

The old time religion faded in the face of the Industrial Revolution and the American Civil War. A new era of Gospel hymns, sung in the churches in the cities began. However the old style of singing endured in the southern states.

CHAPTER EIGHT

THE THIRD GREAT AWAKENING, PART ONE

The American Civil War

This Awakening spanned the period from the late 1850s through to the early twentieth century. Unlike the Second Revival, it was a movement that impacted the cities of the east. However, it was hindered, in the north, at least, by the outbreak of the American Civil War, which lasted from 1861 to 1865. The Confederate armies of the South, on the other hand, experienced their own revival. According to the Confederate chaplain J. William Jones, by the end of the war, 150,000 soldiers had been converted. Generals Stonewall Jackson and Robert E. Lee, both devout Christians, actively supported the revival.

Arguably the most famous song to come out of the Civil War was "Battle Hymn of the Republic," also known as "Mine Eyes Have Seen the Glory." This song was written specifically for the Union armies of the North by Julia Ward Howe, a writer, social activist and anti-slavery campaigner. The tune originated in the camp meeting circuit of the late 1700s and early 1800s.

The hymn has openly Christian lyrics, and is still widely sung in churches and patriotic gatherings to this day.

"Battle Hymn of the Republic"

The late 1800s was a time of rapid industrial growth and immigration. The population of the United States grew from 31 million in 1860 to 106 million in 1920. It was also a time when traditional Christianity was being challenged by a variety of new doctrines, from Andrew Carnegie's gospel of wealth, through Marxism and Darwinism, to the higher Biblical criticism that was emanating from German universities.

William Booth (1829 - 1912) and the Salvation Army

In England, William and Catherine Booth founded the Salvation Army in 1865. Booth loved singing, and his use of the Salvation Army brass band revolutionised the use of instruments in Christian worship.

Booth believed that "hymns" were too churchy. So he used secular songs and put Christian words to them. If

William Booth

someone knew "Here's to Good Ole Whiskey" they could sing "Storm the Forts of Darkness." Many of the songs had catchy titles, like "There are no Flies on Jesus." When he was criticised for using secular tunes to attract crowds, he replied, "Secular music, do you say, belongs to the devil? Does it? Well, if it did I would plunder him for it, for he has no right to a single note of the whole seven." Booth himself wrote several Gospel songs.

"Storm the Forts of Darkness"

At age 13, William Booth was apprenticed to a pawnbroker, in Nottingham. His father, who by Booth's definition was "A Grab, a Get," died the following year. At age 15, however, Booth attended a local Wesleyan chapel and was converted. He vowed that "God shall have all there is of William Booth."

Booth was highly impacted by the visit of an American revivalist named James Caughey. He and a group of friends set out to evangelise the poor through the use of open-air meetings, a technique that would later be employed by the Salvation Army worldwide.

Although he became a Reformed Methodist pastor, he found the "settled ministry" not to his liking and soon resigned. In the meantime he had married Catherine Mumford. The pair was to become a formidable force in the battle for souls.

By 1865, he was back preaching to the poor on the streets of London. His motto was "Go for souls, and go for the worst!" He founded the East London Christian Mission, which, in 1878, became the Salvation Army.

The Army was organised along military lines, with Booth at the top as the "General." He said, "While women weep, as they do now, I'll fight; while children go hungry, as they do now I'll fight; while men go to prison, in and out, in and out, as they do now, I'll fight; while there is a drunkard left, while there is a poor lost girl upon the streets, while there remains one dark soul without the light of God, I'll fight, I'll fight to the very end!"

The Salvation Army drew much opposition, both from the churched and the unchurched. On a number of occasions, hooligans attacked the Salvationists, killing several and wounding many others. A local builder named Charles Frye offered the services of himself and his three sons as bodyguards. All four played brass instruments, so during the marches, they would play their instruments. This proved to be a great attraction, and was the genesis of the Salvation Army band.

The first Salvation Army Band, formed by Charles Frye and his sons in 1882.

From 1896, Booth's son Herbert ministered in Australia. He was responsible for producing *Soldiers of the Cross,* an illustrated lecture combining photographic glass slides with short dramatised film segments and music.

It is estimated William Booth travelled eight million kilometres and preached 60,000 sermons in his 60 years of ministry. This included five trips to the United States and Canada, three to Australia and South Africa, two to India, one to Japan and several to the various European countries. Upon his death in 1912, sixteen thousand officers were serving in his Army.[43]

Moody and Sankey

While Booth was evangelising in Britain, Dwight L. Moody was doing the same in the United States. In 1871, Moody teamed up with singer/songwriter Ira Sankey. From his experience as a successful shoe salesman, Moody pioneered tech-

---

43   "William Bramwell Booth: His Life and Ministry," <http://www.gospeltruth.net/booth/boothbioshort.htm>.

niques of modern mass evangelism that would later be used by others, such as Billy Sunday and Billy Graham.

Before holding a crusade, he would enlist support from all denominations and from local business communities. A house-to-house canvass of residents would be held and a large building rented. Moody knew the value of song in attracting an audience and preparing their hearts to receive the Gospel message. Sankey would sing both before the message, and afterwards while those wishing to repent would be making their way to the inquiry room – another innovation of the Moody Crusades.

Alternating between Europe and America, Moody and Sankey held numerous evangelistic campaigns before more than 100 million people. At their 1883 Cambridge, England, meetings, seven leading university students, the famous "Cambridge Seven," committed themselves to become missionaries in China (under Hudson Taylor).[44]

D. L. Moody (1837 - 1899)

Dwight L. Moody

D. L. Moody came from a family of nine children. His father died when he was five years old, and Moody was largely self-taught. That did not stop him from progressing rapidly towards his goal of earning $100,000 in the shoe sales business, first in Boston, then in Chicago.

After he became a Christian, at 18 years of age, his priorities changed, and he involved himself more and more in Sunday School ministry and in the YMCA. His vision was to help disadvantaged youth from the inner city slums, and in this he was very successful. In 1862, he married Emma Revell, and the couple had three children. He started a church to cater for his growing Sunday School population, but in October 1871, the Great Chicago Fire destroyed the church

---

[44] "Dwight L. Moody: Revivalist with a Common Touch," <http://www.christianitytoday.com/history/people/evangelistsandapologists/dwight-l-moody.html>.

building, his own family dwelling, and the homes of most of his church members. Moody believed that he had saved nothing but his reputation, his family and his Bible.

After the fire, Moody settled on a farm he had bought in Northfield, Massachusetts. He later organised summer conferences which were led and attended by prominent Christian preachers and evangelists from around the world. It was also in Northfield that Moody founded a boys' school and a girls' school, which later merged into today's co-educational, nondenominational Northfield Mount Hermon School.

In 1872, he made the first of a number of visits to the United Kingdom. Soon he was preaching regularly to audiences of 10,000 – 20,000 people. Back in the United States he was much in demand and travelled widely.

As part of his vision for training ordinary people in evangelism, he commenced what became known as the Moody Bible Institute in 1886. Before his death in 1899, he appointed Rev. R. A. Torrey to head up the Institute.

It has been said that "For sanity, sincerity, spirituality, and success Moody goes into the very first rank of revival preachers."[45]

Ira D. Sankey (1840 - 1908)

As a young man, Sankey served in the American Civil War. He often helped the unit chaplain and led his fellow soldiers in hymn singing. After the war, he joined the Internal Revenue Service, and also worked with the Young Men's Christian Association (YMCA). He became well known as a Gospel singer, and eventually came to the attention of D. L. Moody.

It took some persuading before Sankey agreed to give up his well-paid job to join

Ira Sankey

---

[45] "Dwight Lyman Moody: Evangelist," <http://www.wholesomewords.org/biography/biomoody3.html>.

Moody, but by the end of the century, the two were inseparably joined in public esteem.

During the Great Chicago Fire, while Moody was busy helping his neighbours escape the flames, Sankey was gathering up his personal possessions and rowing them to safety in the middle of Lake Michigan. We should not read too much into this, but perhaps it does tell us something about the different characters of the two men.

Sankey always accompanied himself on a small reed organ. While ministering in Edinburgh, the story is told of a Scottish woman who, on hearing Sankey's "Chest o' whistles," shouted "Let me oot! Let me oot! What would John Knox think of the like of ye!"[46]

Sankey was blind for the last five years of his life. In his blindness he found consolation in the friendship of the blind Gospel song writer, Fanny Crosby.

Gospel Hymns

While Psalms and hymns had been the typical musical expression of the First Great Awakening, and folk songs and spirituals of the Second, the urban Gospel song (or Gospel hymn) was the typical genre of the Third Great Awakening. The Gospel song was tuneful, easy to sing, and specifically aimed at converting souls to Christ. It usually took the form of a series of verses, with a repeating chorus.

Ira Sankey wrote many Gospel songs, and he also popularised the songs of other composers, including Philip Bliss and Fanny Crosby. In 1873, Sankey and Bliss collaborated to publish a hymnal called *Sacred Songs and Solos*. The *Gospel Hymn* series followed, with millions of copies being sold in many languages. The Sankey songbooks are still in use today.

One of Sankey's most popular songs is "The Ninety and Nine." In 1874, Moody and Sankey were travelling by train from Glasgow to Edinburgh, Scotland, for some special meetings. One the way, Sankey came across a poem by Elizabeth C. Clephane in a newspaper he was reading. He cut the poem from the paper

---

[46]   John Knox, of course, was a Calvinist preacher, who founded the Scottish Presbyterian Church. The Presbyterians were accustomed to singing only Psalms at this time.

and put it away. Later in the week, Moody had been preaching on the subject of the Good Shepherd. He turned to Sankey and asked if he had an appropriate song to sing. Sankey felt an urging to sing the poem he had found in the newspaper, although it had no tune. As he started playing, and singing the words of the poem, the tune came to him, line by line. It told the story of the Lost Sheep (Luke 15:4-6). The song has remained substantially the same ever since.

 "The Ninety and Nine." It is possible to hear an original recording of Ira Sankey himself singing this song. Go to YouTube, or http://www.sermonaudio.com/sermoninfo.asp?SID=97081010204

Another song, for which Sankey wrote both words and music, is "Out of the Shadowland." It was written especially for Moody's memorial service in Carnegie Hall.

Out of the shadow-land, into the sunshine,
Cloudless, eternal, that fades not away;
Softly and tenderly Jesus will call us;
Home, where the ransom'd are gath'ring to-day.

Chorus:
Silently, peacefully, angels will bear us
Into the beautiful mansions above;
There shall we rest from earth's toiling forever,
Safe in the arms of God's infinite love.

 "Out of the Shadow-Land"

Fanny Crosby (1820 -1915)

The traditional story is that medical malpractice left Fanny Crosby blind at the age of six weeks. Some scientists believe, however, that she may have been congenitally blind.[47] Despite her blindness, Crosby grew up a happy child. In her own words:

> O what a happy soul am I!
> Although I cannot see,
> I am resolved that in this world
> Contented I will be.

At 15, she entered the New York Institute for the Blind, eventually becoming a teacher there. She wrote a number of secular songs, and at least five cantatas, but she is best remembered for her Gospel songs. Many have called her the "Queen of Gospel Song Writers."

Although she had a religious upbringing, Crosby did not experience definite conversion to Christianity until the age of 31. At age 38, she married fellow blind musician and teacher, Alexander van Alstyne, Jr. The couple had one baby girl, who died in her sleep soon after birth. The marriage was unusual, in that Fanny and "Van" lived apart much of the time. Van Alstyne died in 1902.

Crosby worked for a number of publishers, including William B. Bradbury[48] and Biglow and Main Co. At one stage, she was contracted to write three Gospel songs per week. Because some publishers were hesitant to have so many hymns by one person in their hymnals, Crosby used nearly 200 different pseudonyms during her career.

Fanny Crosby

---

[47] "Fanny Crosby: The Early Years," *Leben: A Journal of Reformation Life*, Vol. 4, No. 3, July–September 2008.

[48] William Bradbury (1816-68) wrote the popular tunes for hymns such as "Jesus Loves Me," "Just as I Am," and "Sweet Hour of Prayer."

The tunes for her songs were also written by a number of people, especially W. Howard Doane. Between 1871 and 1908, Crosby worked closely with Ira Sankey, who introduced her songs to a global audience.

Later in her life, Crosby worked at a number of city rescue missions. Much of her income was donated to these causes. She was also active in the Women's Christian Temperance Union.

It is estimated that Fanny Crosby wrote about 8,000 Gospel songs. Many of the songs are still sung today.

 Listen to, or sing, some of the following songs by Fanny Crosby.

"Blessed Assurance"

"To God be the Glory"

"Pass Me Not O Gentle Saviour"

"All the Way My Saviour Leads Me"

"He Hideth My Soul"

"Safe in the Arms of Jesus"

"Tell Me the Story of Jesus"

Philip P. Bliss (1838 - 1876)

Philip Bliss

Born in a log cabin, Philip Bliss had little formal education. He left home at 11 years of age and worked in timber camps and sawmills. Later, he completed his teaching qualifications and became a schoolmaster in Hartford, New York.

In 1858, William B. Bradbury persuaded Bliss to become a music teacher. He subsequently worked as a singing school teacher, travelling from community to community with a melodeon and an old horse.

His wife, Lucy, whom he married in 1859, encouraged Bliss in the development of his talent. A loan of $30 from Lucy's mother enabled Bliss to attend the Normal Academy of Music of New York for six weeks.

The Blisses moved to Chicago in 1864, when Philip was 26. For the next eight years, between 1865 and 1873, often with his wife by his side, he held musical conventions, singing schools, and sacred concerts. In 1869, he formed an association with D. L. Moody. Moody offered him the position of musical director, but Bliss declined, and the job went to Ira Sankey. It was during this time, however, that Bliss wrote many of the Gospel songs for which he would become famous.

In 1874, Bliss decided to commit himself to fulltime evangelical work, little knowing that he had only two and a half more years to live.

On 29 December 1876, he and his wife were involved in a train crash. Bliss escaped from the train, but went back into the burning carriage to try and rescue Lucy. Neither of their bodies was ever found. They left two sons, aged four and one.

In her autobiography *Memories of Eighty Years*, Fanny Crosby makes the following statement.

The night before that terrible railroad accident at Ashtabula…he [Bliss] said to his audience, "I may not pass this way again"; then he sang a solo, "I'm Going Home Tomorrow." This indeed proved prophetic of his own home going.[49]

Philip. P. Bliss is generally regarded as one of the greatest Gospel song writers. Many of his songs are still sung today.

Listen to, or sing, some of the following songs by Philip Bliss.
"It Is Well with My Soul" (Bliss wrote the music for this famous song)
"Hallelujah, What a Saviour"

---

[49] Fanny J. Crosby, *Memories of Eighty Years*, James H. Earle and Co., Boston, 1906, p. 137.

"Dare To Be a Daniel"
"Jesus Loves Even Me"
"Wonderful Words of Life"

"It Is Well with My Soul"

Many people know the story behind this famous song, which was written by Horatio Spafford. On November 22, 1873, the ship *Ville du Havre* was lost on the voyage between the United States and France. On board were Spafford's wife Anna, and their four daughters. The ship sank rapidly, with the loss of 226 passengers and crew, including the four girls. Anna alone survived.

Spafford, who had been detained by business, immediately set sail for Britain to bring his wife home. On the Atlantic crossing, the captain of his ship called Spafford to his cabin to tell him that they were passing over the spot where his four daughters had died. Later, Spafford wrote the lyrics for "It Is Well With My Soul." He asked his good friend, Philip Bliss, to write the music. Bliss named the tune VILLE DU HAVRE.

Other Gospel Songwriters

There were many other Gospel songwriters of this era.

- Elisha A. Hoffman (1839 – 1929) – a Presbyterian minister who wrote about 2,000 songs, including "Leaning on the Everlasting Arms" and "Are You Washed in the Blood?"

 "Are You Washed in the Blood?"

- Robert Lowry (1826 – 1899) – Lowry was a professor of literature, and later chancellor, of Bucknell University, Lewisburg. He was also a Baptist minister and Gospel song writer. He wrote about 500 songs, including "Nothing but the Blood," "Low in the Grave He Lay," and "Shall We Gather at the River." He also wrote the tune and chorus for Isaac Watts' hymn "We're Marching to Zion."

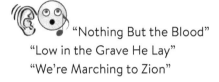 "Nothing But the Blood"
"Low in the Grave He Lay"
"We're Marching to Zion"

- Daniel B. Towner (1850 – 1919) and John H. Sammis (1846 – 1919) - In 1887, just after an evangelistic meeting held by D. L. Moody, a young man stood to share his story in an after-service testimony meeting. It was clear that he knew little about Christian doctrine, but his closing words – "I'm not quite sure – but I'm going to trust, and I'm going to obey" - impacted Daniel B. Towner. Towner was working for Moody at the time, conducting the music and singing songs. He wrote down the young man's words and gave them to John Sammis, a Presbyterian minister, who developed the lyrics for the song "Trust and Obey." Towner wrote the tune. This song gives a simple, clear expression of the Christian walk.

 "Trust and Obey"

- Joseph Scriven (1819 – 1886) – Joseph Scriven was born in Ireland. After losing his fiancée by drowning the night before his wedding, he moved to Canada. A member of the Plymouth Brethren Church, he was known for doing good works, but was regarded as a bit eccentric. Eventually, he fell in love again, but, sadly, his fiancée died from pneumonia just before the wedding. In 1886, he drowned in a watercourse.

He was depressed at the time, so it is not known if the drowning was accidental or suicide. Some time before his death, he wrote a poem to comfort his sick mother in Ireland. The poem was called "Pray Without Ceasing." Eventually the poem was put to music by Charles Converse, and became the well-loved hymn "What a Friend We Have in Jesus."

 "What a Friend We Have in Jesus"

- Frances Ridley Havergal (1836 – 1879) - Havergal was a bright but short-lived candle in English hymnody. She was reading by age four, and began writing verse at age seven. She learned Latin, Greek and Hebrew, as well as several modern languages, and she memorised the Psalms, the book of Isaiah, and most of the New Testament. During her lifetime, she published several volumes of poems and hymns. She was also much involved in charitable work. Never in very good health, she died from peritonitis at the age of 42. Havergal's well-known songs include "Take My Life and Let It Be," "Like a River Glorious," and "Who Is on the Lord's Side."

 "Take My Life and Let It Be" (This song has a number of different tunes. Try NOTTINGHAM, which is attributed to W. A. Mozart.)

- Cecil Frances ("Fanny") Alexander (1818 – 1895) was an Irish hymn-writer. Her father encouraged her to write poems, and at the age of 30, she published *Hymns for Little Children*. This book contained the well-loved songs "There Is a Green Hill Far Away," "All Things Bright and Beautiful," and "Once in Royal David's City." By the end of the nineteenth century, this book had gone through 69 editions. In 1850, she married William Alexander, who later became Archbishop of Armagh. The couple had two sons and two daughters. During her lifetime Alexander was known for her devotion to the poor, mentally handicapped, the deaf and the sick.

 "All Things Bright and Beautiful"
"There Is a Green Hill Far Away"

- Johnson Oatman Jnr. (1856 – 1922) – Oatman was an ordained minister in the Methodist Episcopal Church, but he worked full-time in the retail and insurance industries. He wrote the lyrics for about 5,000 Gospel songs, including "Count Your Blessings" and "Higher Ground."

 "Count Your Blessings"
"Higher Ground" (This may be sung to the Charles Gabriel tune HIGHER GROUND. It is also often sung to the Fijian folk tune "Isa Lei.")

- James M. Black (1856 – 1938) – Black attended the Pine Street Methodist Episcopal Church in Williamsport, Pennsylvania, from 1904 until his death, serving as a song leader and Sunday school teacher. He wrote about 1,500 Gospel songs, his most famous one being "When the Roll Is called Up Yonder." The story is told that, one day in 1893, Black was calling the roll for a youth meeting. Young Bessie, daughter of a drunkard, did not show up, and he was disappointed at her failure to appear. Black made a comment to the effect, "Well, I trust when the roll is called up yonder, she'll be there." He tried to respond with an appropriate song, but could not find one in his song book:

This lack of a fitting song caused me both sorrow and disappointment. An inner voice seemed to say, "Why don't you write one?" I put away the thought. As I opened the gate on my way home, the same thought came again so strongly that tears filled my eyes. I entered the house and sat down at the piano. The words came to me effortlessly…The tune came the same way—I dared not change a single note or word.

"When the Roll is Called Up Yonder"

• Ada Ruth Habershon (1861 – 1918) – Habershon was an English hymnist associated with Charles Spurgeon. She met D. L. Moody and Ira Sankey during their 1881 preaching tour of Britain. At their prompting, she visited the United States and delivered a series of lectures on Old Testament typology, which were later published. In 1905, Charles Alexander and R. A. Torrey toured Britain, and Alexander asked Habershon to write some hymns for use during the tour. She eventually sent him 200 hymns, but only one of them is commonly sung today. "Will the Circle Be Unbroken" was originally a Christian song, but the Carter family changed it into a story about the death, funeral and mourning of the narrator's mother in 1935.

 "Will the Circle Be Unbroken"

CHAPTER NINE

THE THIRD GREAT AWAKENING, PART TWO

Revival!

During the 1890s, there was a widespread expectation that God was going to move in a new and exciting way. A worldwide movement at that time was praying specifically for revival.

In America, Rev. R.A. Torrey had been called to head up what became known as the Moody Bible Institute in Chicago. Regular prayer meetings were held every Saturday night, and these sometimes extended right through to the early hours of Sunday morning. At one of these meetings, Torrey was led by the Spirit to pray that he would be released to preach the Gospel throughout the world, and that thousands would come to know Christ as their Saviour.

Soon after, representatives from Victoria, Australia, arrived, requesting him to evangelise their country. They had hoped to have Moody himself, but he had died in 1899.

Torrey ministered successfully in Australia and New Zealand in 1902 with the song leader, Charles Alexander (author of the famous red hymnbook *Alexander's Hymns*). As they toured, many were won to Christ. Gospel songs became so popular that you could hear them sung in shops and factories and whistled in the streets. Some businesses actually closed so that staff members could attend the meetings. Alexander stated that "I look at a Gospel song as a sermon – a sermon on wheels, and when you teach a good Gospel song to a man, it is like starting a wagon down a hill with the brakes off."[50]

In 1909, Charles Alexander once again toured Australia, this time with the American Presbyterian minister, J. Wilbur Chapman. A second tour, in 1912-13 also included New Zealand.

Probably the most popular song of the Alexander crusades was "The Glory Song." The words and music were written by Charles Gabriel. Alexander did not like the song at first, but when he heard it sung, he changed his mind. "It took such a hold of me that I could think of nothing else for days thereafter. I got my friends to sing it. I dreamed about it, and woke to the rhythm of it. Then I began to teach it to large audiences, and soon whole towns were ringing with the melody." This was to be become the most popular song of the 1904-05 Welsh Revival.

 "The Glory Song"

One of the outstanding results of the revival movement in the early years of the twentieth century was the boost given to local temperance movements. Some places actually voted to ban the sale of alcohol as a result of the influence of Christianity. The temperance movement also reinforced the women's suffrage movement.

Charles M. Alexander (1867 - 1920)

"Charlie," as he was known to thousands who attended the great revival crusades of R. A. Torrey and J. Wilbur Chapman, was a gifted musician. His mother read Moody's sermons to her children around the fire at night, and Alexander was converted at age 13.

Charles Alexander

---

50 George T. Davis, *Twice around the World with Alexander*, The Christian Herald, New York, 1907, p. 352.

In 1904, Alexander married Helen Cadbury, daughter of the president of Cadbury Chocolate Company. She toured with him on the evangelistic circuit as a women's worker. Together they spread The Pocket Testament League around the world.

Helen Alexander wrote the lyrics for the hymn "Anywhere With Jesus," while Daniel Towner wrote the tune.

Billy Sunday and Homer Rodeheaver

Until Billy Graham, no American evangelist preached to so many millions, or saw as many conversions as Billy Sunday — an estimated 300,000. With Homer Rodeheaver as his music director, Sunday hit the "kerosene circuit" [51] for the first two decades of the twentieth century.

Billy Sunday crusades were quite different to those of D. L. Moody and Ira Sankey. While Moody and Sankey favoured more serious sentimental songs, or songs that emphasised humility (for example, "Oh, To Be Nothing," by Georgiana Taylor), the Sunday/Rodeheaver songs were lively, entertaining and militant ("Onward Christian Soldiers," "Battle Hymn of the Republic"). Warfare was an important part of a Sunday crusade. In the songbook that Rodeheaver compiled and published, there was a whole section on Warfare.

Billy Sunday crusades were entertaining. Rodeheaver was a showman, and he liked to use show biz methods. Sunday was also a showman. A typical crusade meeting would start with half an hour of singing – first well-known songs, then new songs. Of course, the new songs soon became popular, so that created a market for Rodeheaver's songbooks and sound recordings (which soon outsold printed music). This laid the foundations of twentieth century "American Christian culture" (now international).

---

[51] So called because most of the communities that he ministered to did not yet have electric power.

Billy Sunday (1862 - 1935)

Billy Sunday was born into poverty. His parents were German immigrants who had changed their name from Sonntag to Sunday. His father died of pneumonia in the Union Army soon before Billy's birth. Billy spent much of his childhood with his grandfather and in the Iowa Soldiers' Orphans' Home.

Billy Sunday

One of his first jobs was as a stable boy for Colonel John Scott. The Scotts treated him well and sent him to secondary school, where he excelled in athletics. In 1883, he was signed by the Chicago White Stockings baseball team, and went on to spend the next eight years in the major leagues.

In 1886, after hearing a group from the Chicago Pacific Garden Mission preaching on the street, Sunday gave his life to God. Following his conversion, he changed his behaviour, denouncing drinking, swearing and gambling. Two years later he married Helen "Nell" Thompson.

His first job in Christian service was with the YMCA. Then he worked as full-time assistant to J. Wilbur Chapman, during the latter's evangelistic tours. When Chapman unexpectedly returned to the pastorate in 1896, Sunday struck out on his own.

In the early years, he mainly ministered in smaller centres. The local community would erect a large, temporary wooden "Tabernacle," with a sawdust floor. Those who wanted to give their lives to Christ were invited to "hit the sawdust trail."

Sunday's preaching was unconventional. He used slang and colloquialisms. He also made full use of his athletic ability. To quote a newspaper of the day, "Sunday was a whirling dervish that pranced and cavorted and strode and bounded and pounded all over his platform and left them thrilled and bewildered as they have never been before."

His sermons on sexual sin were remarkably explicit for the time. He reserved his greatest condemnation, however, for the liquor trade. His preaching played a large role in getting Prohibition passed in the 1920s. He supported women's suffrage and included Afro-Americans in his revivals, even when he toured the Deep South.

From 1908, Sunday's wife, Nell, toured with him and managed his campaigns. She hired staff, including Homer Rodeheaver, who was Sunday's musical director for 20 years between 1910 and 1930. Nell was also an accomplished speaker and writer. She spoke at some of the early Billy Graham crusades, before her own death in 1957.

Sadly, the Sundays' three sons, who had been largely reared by strangers, rebelled against their parents and engaged in the very activities that Sunday was preaching against. All three died in tragic circumstances. Their eldest child, Helen, developed multiple sclerosis, and died of pneumonia in 1932.

During the course of his lifetime, Sunday probably preached to about 100 million people face-to-face, usually without electronic amplification.

Homer Rodeheaver (1880 - 1955)

Homer Rodeheaver

Called "Rody" by associates and reporters alike, Homer Rodeheaver was a friendly and genial man, with a rich baritone voice and a talent for playing the trombone. He had a great stage presence, and was adept at winning over an audience with a practical joke, a magic trick, a funny story, or some strange noises on his trombone. In the days before electronic amplification, he used the trombone to lead the people in singing.

In 1910, Rodeheaver established his own publishing company, The Rodeheaver Company. He also recorded over 500 songs on many different record labels in the course of his career. In 1922, his company began producing 78-rpm recordings on its own Rainbow label. This is generally regarded as the first exclusively Gospel recording label.

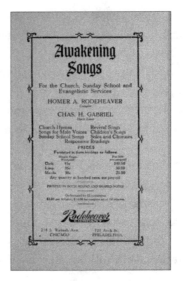

This songbook, *Awakening Songs*, was published
by The Rodeheaver Company in 1917.

Although Rodeheaver wrote a number of Gospel songs, he also made use of
the talents of other song writers and composers.

You can hear an original audio clip of Homer Rodeheaver singing on
YouTube, or at www.sermonaudio.com.

Other Gospel Songwriters

- Charles H. Gabriel (1856 – 1932) –
  Growing up on an Iowa farm, Gabriel
  taught himself to play the family's
  reed organ. He began teaching in singing schools by age 16, and became well
  known as a teacher and composer. He

Charles H. Gabriel

served as music director at a number of churches before starting work with Homer Rodeheaver's publishing company in 1912. He wrote "The Glory Song" and the music for "Higher Ground."

"Brighten the Corner Where You Are" – This became the theme song for the Billy Sunday Crusades. The music was written by Gabriel, and the words by Ina Ogdon. Ogdon wanted to be an evangelist, but her father's illness forced her to abandon those plans. She wrote encouraging words to show how one can serve the Lord in different ways and circumstances. "Brighten the Corner" was criticised for its lack of an overtly Christian message, but Rodeheaver replied that it was not intended for a Sunday morning church service or a devotional meeting. Its purpose was to bridge the gap between the popular song of the day and the great hymns and gospel songs.

"His Eye Is on the Sparrow" – Gabriel wrote the music and Civilla D. Martin wrote the lyrics. She and her husband were visiting friends – the wife was bed-ridden and the husband was a cripple. She asked them how they coped and the wife replied "his eye is on the sparrow and I know he watches me." Ethel Waters made this song famous in the Billy Graham Crusades and it became the title for her autobiography.

"I Stand Amazed in the Presence" (words and music)

"In Loving-kindness Jesus Came" (words and music)

"Since Jesus Came into My Heart" – Gabriel wrote the music and Rufus McDaniel wrote the lyrics after the death of his son in 1914.

• George Bennard (1873 – 1958) – As a young man, Bennard wanted to become an evangelist, but when his father died unexpectedly, he was forced to support his mother and sister. Later, he preached throughout the United States and Canada for the Salvation Army, and was ordained as a Methodist Episcopal minister. He wrote a number of songs, which were published by The Rodeheaver Company. The most famous song was "The Old Rugged Cross."

"The Old Rugged Cross"

- Oswald J. Smith (1889 – 1986) – Oswald J. Smith has been described as one of the most versatile leaders in the history of the Christian church.[52] Over 80 years, he preached more than 12,000 sermons in 80 countries, wrote 35 books and 1,200 poems and hymns. He was founding pastor of The People's Church in Toronto, Canada. He had a heart for mission work, and raised much money and many recruits for that ministry. After 1930, he collaborated with B. D. Ackley, who wrote the music for a number of Smith's songs. The songs were published by The Rodeheaver Company. In 1939, Rodeheaver supplied the music for a song describing the change that becoming a Christian made in a person's life. This became the famous song "Then Jesus Came."

 "Then Jesus Came"

- Austin Miles (1868 – 1946) – Austin Miles gave up his job as a pharmacist to write Gospel songs. He served as editor and manager at the Hall-Mack Company, which was taken over by The Rodeheaver Company in 1936. Miles wrote just under 400 Gospel songs. The most famous of these are "In the Garden," "Wide, Wide as the Ocean," and "Dwelling in Beulah Land." These are songs that were used by Rodeheaver.

.

 "In the Garden"
"Dwelling in Beulah Land" (Based on Isaiah 62:4)
"Wide, Wide as the Ocean"

---

52 "Oswald Jeffrey Smith, Pastor, Evangelist," <http://www.believersweb.org/view.cfm?ID=130>.

The Story of "In the Garden"

I read...the story of the greatest morn in history: "The first day of the week cometh Mary Magdalene early, while it was yet very dark, unto the sepulchre." Instantly, completely, there unfolded in my mind the scenes of the garden of Joseph....Out of the mists of the garden comes a form, halting, hesitating, tearful, seeking, turning from side to side in bewildering amazement. Falteringly, bearing grief in every accent, with tear-dimmed eyes, she whispers, "If thou hast borne him hence"... "He speaks, and the sound of His voice is so sweet the birds hush their singing." Jesus said to her, "Mary!" Just one word from his lips, and forgotten the heartaches, the long dreary hours....all the past blotted out in the presence of the Living Present and the Eternal Future.

- Lewis E. Jones (1865 – 1936) – Lewis Jones was a classmate of Billy Sunday at Moody Bible Institute. After graduation, he worked for the YMCA. "Power in the Blood" was written at a camp meeting in 1899.

 "Power in the Blood"

- Helen H. Lemmel (1863 - 1961) – Helen Lemmel became a vocal music teacher at the Moody Bible Institute in Chicago, Illinois. Among her works are a hymnal used by evangelist Billy Sunday for over a decade. Lemmel and a women's choral group she directed were part of Sunday's team at the peak of his career.

 "Turn Your Eyes Upon Jesus"

- Eliza Hewitt (1851-1920) – After becoming a teacher, Eliza Hewitt was confined to bed for a time with spinal problems, possibly caused by being struck in the back with a heavy slate by a rebellious schoolboy. While in bed, she wrote many well-loved Gospel songs, and worked with other songwriters such as Charles Gabriel and Homer Rodeheaver. She was also friends with Fanny Crosby. The song "Sunshine in My Soul" was written when she was able to go for a walk in the park after being in a body cast for six months.

 "When We All Get to Heaven"
"Sunshine in My Soul"
"More about Jesus"

- Thoro Harris (1874 - 1955) – Thoro Harris is famous for composing the song "He's Coming Soon." The tune that is most commonly used for this song was composed by Queen Liliuokalani (1838-1917), the last monarch and only Queen of Hawaii. It was written in 1877, and is known as "Aloha 'Oe" ("Farewell to Thee"). Harris also wrote "All that Thrills My Soul" ("Who Can Cheer the Heart Like Jesus") in 1931.

 "He's Coming Soon"

The Beginnings of Pentecostalism

The modern day Pentecostal Movement, with its emphasis on the "baptism in the Holy Spirit" and "speaking in tongues" really began in the early years of the twentieth century, at a time when many nations were experiencing spiritual revival.

In 1900, Charles Fox Parham started Bethel Bible College in Topeka, Kansas. Parham challenged his students to read the book of Acts and find an answer to the question, "What is the evidence that a person has been baptised in the Holy

Spirit?" When his students came back together again, they all agreed that the evidence was "speaking in other tongues." Agnes Ozman, one of the students, received the baptism and spoke in Chinese on New Year's Day, 1901. Soon many others had this experience.

A young black student, William J. Seymour, took this teaching back to Los Angeles and started meetings in a former stable on Azusa Street. His following grew and many people poured in for this Holy Ghost revival. The revival ran from 1906 to 1913, and from there it spread worldwide.

The Azusa Street Faith Mission is considered to be the
birth-place of the Pentecostal movement.

To begin with, the mainstream denominations rejected this outpouring of the Holy Spirit, and Spirit-filled believers were often excluded from membership. As a result, about 300 people met in Hot Springs, Arkansas, in 1914 to form the Assemblies of God Church, which has since become the world's largest Pentecostal movement.

Azusa Street was integrated, but soon the movement split into white and black churches – white churches became known as "Pentecostal," while the black churches were "Holiness" churches.

Frank Bartleman's Testimony

Frank Bartleman was an early participant in the Azusa Street Revival. He wrote the following Testimony. In it, he laments the commercialisation of Christian music and the loss of the spontaneous "song of the Lord."

In the beginning in "Azusa" we had no musical instruments. In fact we felt no need of them. There was no place for them in our worship. All was spontaneous. We did not even sing from hymnbooks. All the old well-known hymns were sung from memory, quickened by the Spirit of God. "The Comforter Has Come," was possibly the one must sung. We sang it from fresh, powerful heart experience. Oh, how the power of God filled and thrilled us. Then the "blood" songs were very popular. The life is in the blood. Sinai, Calvary, and Pentecost, all had their rightful place in the "Azusa" work. But the "new song" was altogether different, not of human composition. It cannot be successfully counterfeited. The crow cannot imitate the dove. But they finally began to despise this "gift," when the human spirit asserted itself again. They drove it out by hymnbooks, and selected songs by leaders. It was like murdering the Spirit, and most painful to some of us, but the tide was too strong against us. Hymnbooks today are largely a commercial proposition, and we would not lose much without most of them. The old tunes, even, are violated by change, and new styles must be gotten out of every season, for added profit. There is very little real spirit of worship in them. They move the toes, but not the hearts of men. The spirit of song given from God in the beginning was like the Aeolian harp, in its spontaneity and sweetness. In fact it was the very breath of God, playing on human heartstrings, or human vocal cords. The notes were wonderful in sweetness, volume and duration. In fact they were of times humanly impossible. It was "singing in the Spirit."

Frank Bartleman, *How Pentecost Came to Los Angeles: As It Was in the Beginning,* 1925, pp. 57-58. See <http://www.ccel.org/ccel/bartleman/los.i.html>.

Songs that were popular in the Azusa Street Revival included "The Comforter Has Come," "Fill Me Now," "Joy Unspeakable," and "Love Lifted Me."

 "The Comforter Has Come" – written in 1890 by Frank Bottome.
"Fill Me Now" – written in 1879 by Elwood H.Stokes.
"Love Lifted Me" – written in 1912 by James Rowe.
"Joy Unspeakable" – written in 1900 by Barney E. Warren.

"Joy Unspeakable"

I have found His grace is all complete,
He supplieth ev'ry need;
While I sit and learn at Jesus' feet,
I am free, yes, free indeed.

Refrain
It is joy unspeakable and full of glory,
Full of glory, full of glory,
It is joy unspeakable and full of glory,
Oh, the half has never yet been told.

Missionaries took the Pentecostal message all over the world. Today there are over 500 million Pentecostal and charismatic Christians worldwide – second only to the Roman Catholics.

It is impossible to overemphasise the contribution of Azusa Street to the development of Christian music. Pentecostalism in general released a new freedom of the Holy Spirit into worship. Many instruments that had previously been unacceptable in mainstream churches became part of the Pentecostal experience. Holiness churches, in particular, "served as a leader and catalyst in bringing new forms of music into the black church, including the addition of musical instruments, once considered 'of the Devil' because they made the music sound 'worldly' or like contemporary secular music."[53]

SECULAR TO SACRED

Many secular melodies have had Christian words added to them. These are five that have achieved international fame.

- "Be Still My Soul" – Little is known of the German woman Katharina A. von Schlegel. She may have been involved in the German Pietist movement of the 1700s. She wrote the lyrics to this hymn in 1752, and they were translated into English by Jane Borthwick in 1855. The most popular version of this hymn is based on the tune "Finlandia" (1899) by the patriotic Finnish composer, Jean Sibelius. This was reportedly the favourite hymn of the athlete, Eric Liddell.

    At least five other Christian songs have been set to the same tune. One of them is called "We Rest on Thee." This version is famous because it was the last hymn sung by the five American missionaries massacred by Auca Indians in the Amazon in 1956. The last verse of the hymn gave the title to Elisabeth Elliot's book *Through Gates of Splendor*.

    > We rest on Thee, our shield and our defender!
    > Thine is the battle, Thine shall be the praise;
    > When passing through the gates of pearly splendor,

---

[53] Cusic, *op. cit.*, p. 122.

Victors, we rest with Thee, through endless days.
When passing through the gates of pearly splendor,
Victors, we rest with Thee, through endless days.

 "Be Still My Soul"

- "Joyful, Joyful, We Adore Thee" - Henry van Dyke (1852 – 1933) was a Presbyterian clergyman and author. He wrote the poem "Joyful, Joyful, We Adore Thee" in 1907 to go with the music "Ode to Joy" from the Fourth Movement of Beethoven's Ninth (Choral) Symphony. This was the first major symphony to employ human voices, and Beethoven wrote it when he was almost completely deaf. Van Dyke said of the hymn: "These verses are simple expressions of common Christian feelings and desires in this present time— hymns of today that may be sung together by people who know the thought of the age, and are not afraid that any truth of science will destroy religion, or any revolution on earth overthrow the kingdom of heaven. Therefore this is a hymn of trust and joy and hope."

 "Joyful, Joyful, We Adore Thee"

- "I Cannot Tell" - William Young Fullerton (1857 - 1932) was born in Belfast, Ireland. He moved to London as a young man and came into contact with Charles Spurgeon, who became his friend and mentor. Fullerton went on to become a popular speaker at Keswick Conventions. He served as President of the Baptist Union and Home Secretary of the Baptist Missionary Society. The song for which he is most famous is "I Cannot Tell." He wrote this in 1929, to the traditional Irish melody LONDONDERRY AIR. The love song "Danny Boy," also based on the same tune, was written in 1910.

 "I Cannot Tell"

- "Goin' Home" - Antonin Dvorak was a Czech composer who came to the United States between 1892 and 1895. As Director of the National Conservatory of Music of America he taught and composed. Dvorak was very interested in Native American Indian music as well as Negro spirituals. His *Symphony #9 in E minor* was first performed in 1893. Known as the *New World Symphony*, it has become one of the most popular of all classical music compositions, especially the Second Movement, or Largo.

  In 1922, one of his students, William Arms Fisher, put words to the Second Movement and it became the song "Goin' Home." The song is very like a spiritual with its theme of death and going to Heaven.

 "Goin' Home"

- "Search Me, O God" - There is no doubt that J. Edwin Orr was one of last century's greatest preachers and writers on the subject of revival in the church and in society. From an early age, he enjoyed travelling, and by the 1960s, he had visited all except ten of the world's countries, and 500 of the 600 major cities.

  Orr arrived in New Zealand on 6 April 1936, at the age of 24, ready to take part in the Easter Convention at Ngaruawahia. (The Ngaruawahia Convention was an annual convention run along Keswick lines.) On Friday night, the Holy Spirit moved in one of the tents, bringing confession of sin, followed by the joy of deliverance. The noise attracted others from nearby tents. The Saturday evening meeting went on until after midnight, and on Sunday evening, young people crowded the platform to testify of what God had done in their lives. "The meeting concluded with singing such as one expects to hear in heaven," stated one of the organizers.

News of the happenings at Ngaruawahia spread throughout the country and helped prepare the way for Orr's other meetings. The events that took place throughout New Zealand at this time were so marvellous, that they have been recorded in E. Towns' and D. Porter's recent book *The Ten Greatest Revivals of all Time*.

Orr wrote the song "Search Me, O God" in five minutes on the back of an envelope at the Ngaruawahia Convention. It was based on the Maori tune "Now Is the Hour," which was written in the early 1900s.

 "Search Me, O God"

CHAPTER TEN

THE RISE OF BLACK GOSPEL

What Is Gospel?

Gospel music goes by many names. Black Gospel, Southern Gospel, Country Gospel and Celtic Gospel are but four of them. Out of all this Gospel music, however, a new type of song has arisen in recent years. It is known as Contemporary Christian Music, or CCM.

The word "Gospel" is difficult to define. Gospel songs that tell the "Good News" of Jesus Christ are usually emotional and lively, with a simple melody. They commonly feature verses and a repeating chorus, and are accompanied by various musical instruments. "Essentially the gospel songs are songs of testimony, persuasion, religious exhortation, or warning."[54] In the early days, many people, especially in the Southern and Midwestern states of the USA, were unable to read. Songs had to be easy to learn, with plenty of repetition. African-Americans who attended church with their masters learned songs to which they would later put their own spin.

The great crusades of Moody, Chapman and Sunday developed the urban Gospel song (or hymn) written by recognised composers and lyricists. The urban Gospel song was popularised by singers such as Sankey, Alexander and Rodeheaver, and aided by the development of Christian publishing companies that were eager to promote new songs.

---

[54] Charles E. Gold, "The Gospel Song: Contemporary Opinion," *The Hymn*, Vol. 9, No. 3, July 1958, p. 70.

Technological Change

Publishing, however, was overtaken by two new developments of the early twentieth century that revolutionised the distribution of Christian music. The phonograph and the radio turned music from a local event into a national entity. Thomas Edison's phonograph was invented in 1877. At first it used cylinders, then, later, shellac discs. A 12-inch shellac disc, first used in 1903, lasted for about three minutes. So most songs recorded throughout the twentieth century were three minutes long.

Wireless radio was invented by the Italian, Guglielmo Marconi, in 1895. The first broadcasting licence in the United States was issued to station KDKA, in Pittsburgh, Pennsylvania, in November 1920. The following January, the station broadcast a church service from the Calvary Episcopal Church, and this became a regular weekly event.

The period from 1925 to 1950 has been called the Golden Age of radio broadcasting. Radio was the main source of family entertainment until the advent of television.

Black Gospel

Black Gospel is essentially a style of singing. You can take any hymn or Gospel song and make it Black Gospel. We can recognise eight qualities of Black Gospel worship:

- it is emotional
- it involves congregational participation
- it involves call and response
- it uses improvisation
- it uses flatted notes and pentatonic scales
- it is very rhythmic, often with a syncopated beat
- it uses delayed time – off the regular meter
- there is much embellishment of the tune

The musical roots of Black Gospel "can be found in spirituals, work songs, slave songs, white Pentecostal hymns, and evangelistic congregational songs from the seventeenth, eighteenth, and nineteenth centuries."[55]

Between the end of the American Civil War and the early twentieth century, Black Gospel reinvented itself. To begin with, there was a backlash against the traditional music of the slavery period, which many saw as being base and degrading. Black church services became formal, and many African-Americans entered newly-formed black universities, in an effort to "move up" in the world.

The Fisk Jubilee Singers performed the old Spirituals, but they did so in a formal, European style.

Fisk Jubilee Singers

Fisk Jubilee Singers, 1882

Fisk School opened in Nashville in 1866. The following year, it obtained a university charter. From the beginning, however, the university was very short of money. To alleviate this, Fisk's treasurer and music professor, George L. White, decided to tour the university choir, which eventually took on the name Jubilee Singers.

Early tours of the northern states did not raise much money. The singers were often denied transport and accommodation because of the colour of their skin. However, as their fame increased, they began to earn enough funds to expand the university campus. In 1873, they toured England, meeting up with D. L. Moody and singing at several of his meetings.

Further tours followed until the original group was disbanded in 1878. It reformed in 1879, but had become defunct by 1900, when it was resurrected by John Wesley Works and his brother Frederick. As well as leading the group on

---

[55] Trineice Robinson-Martin, "Performance Styles and Musical Characteristics of Black Gospel Music," *Journal of Singing*, Vol. 65, No. 5, May/June 2009.

tours of the United States, the brothers published *New Jubilee Songs* in 1901 and *Folk Songs of the American Negro* in 1907. These books did a lot to keep alive the musical heritage of the African-Americans. The Fisk Jubilee Singers have continued to the present day as a touring ensemble of Fisk University students.

Listen to a recording of the Fisk Jubilee Singers

The Holiness Movement

The Azusa Street Revival was a major catalyst for change in African-American worship; however change had already begun before that. The "Holiness movement" of the late 1800s, flowing out of the Wesleyan movement, taught that an individual could be delivered from the practice of sin and live free from sin in this present world through the power of the Holy Spirit. This process was known as "entire sanctification". It was a definite, datable event that occurred after salvation and cleansed and enabled the believer to live a life of holiness.

The "Holiness movement" and the new "Pentecostal movement" did not always see eye to eye, especially in regards to "speaking in tongues," which was rejected by many Holiness advocates. Those who accepted Pentecostalism (known as Wesleyan Pentecostals) taught that the personal cleansing brought about by entire sanctification prepared the believer to receive the third definite experience of baptism in the Holy Spirit.

Other Pentecostal denominations, such as the Assemblies of God, believed that there were only two definite experiences – conversion and Spirit baptism. Sanctification, they believed, is an ongoing process that occurs throughout a believer's lifetime.

A Baptist minister, Charles Harrison Mason, was expelled from the Baptist denomination for preaching "Holiness." He went on to form the Church of God in Christ (COGIC). In 1906, he came under the influence of Azusa Street and began to speak in tongues.

Bishop C. H. Mason

121

Mason continued as Senior Bishop of COGIC until he died in 1961, at the age of 95. Today, the Church of God in Christ is the largest black Pentecostal denomination in the United States, with 12,000 congregations and about five million members. Several influential Gospel performers, including Andrae Crouch, Edwin Hawkins and BeBe and CeCe Winans, have COGIC roots.

Mason composed several songs, including "Yes Lord" (which became known as the COGIC chant) and "I'm a Soldier in the Army of the Lord."

"I'm a Soldier in the Army of the Lord"
"Yes Lord" (COGIC chant)

Another important figure in the development of Black Gospel was Rev. Dr. Charles Albert Tindley. The son of a slave, Tindley was largely self-educated. He went on to become an influential Methodist minister, civil rights worker and Gospel hymn writer. One of the songs that he composed was called "I'll Overcome Someday." Some claim that this song became the basis for the civil rights anthem, "We Shall Overcome."

"I'll Overcome Someday"

The Black Gospel Quartet

One of the distinctive sounds of Black Gospel is the Black Gospel quartet. The quartet had its origins in the 1890s. While the Dinwiddie Colored Quartet was the first black vocal quartet to record on disc, in 1902, earlier recordings by the Unique Quartette had been made on wax cylinders in 1893.

Early black quartets were mainly of Baptist origin, and they sang in a very formal style. Groups that formed in Holiness and Pentecostal churches, on the other hand, were much freer, with more body movement, improvisation and emotion. Gradually these elements filtered into most of the quartets, forming a distinctly "Black Gospel" sound.

Black Gospel quartets of the early 1900s included the Blue Jay Singers, Silver Leaf Quartet, Dixie Hummingbirds and Fairfield Four. Later on came the Soul Stirrers, Four Harmony Kings and the Golden Gate Quartet. The latter group grew out of the Booker T. Washington High School and, in 1925, it became one of the first quartets to be heard live on the radio.

 Listen to one of the Black Gospel quartets listed above.

The Golden Gate
Quartet in 1964

To begin with, quartets sang a cappella, but the addition of Holiness and Pentecostal singers led to the introduction of musical instruments. One of the first musicians was a blind black pianist called Arizona Dranes. She recorded for Okeh Records in about 1926.

Dranes was a favoured singer-pianist of Bishop Charles Mason, and she was much used in COGIC circles. She incorporated a syncopated, ragtime style into her accompaniment.

 "My Soul is a Witness for My Lord" – Arizona Dranes

Thomas A. Dorsey (1899 – 1993)

By the 1930s, there was a widening gap between the main stream churches and the Holiness/Pentecostal churches, which were creating a new style of worship experience. Their services were filled with emotional ecstasy, dramatic testimonies, dancing, clapping hands and stamping feet. The singing was

Thomas A. Dorsey

forceful and a number of different instruments were used. The music was loud, rhythmic and jubilant, and a song, accompanied by a "shouting session" could last half an hour or more.[56]

The key figure in Black Gospel song writing and publishing was Thomas A. Dorsey. He has been called the "Father of Black Gospel."

Dorsey was born in Georgia in 1899, the son of a Baptist minister. He began his musical career as a secular blues pianist known as "Georgia Tom." After studying music formally in Chicago, he became an agent for Paramount Records.

During the 1920s, he wrote more than 400 jazz and blues songs. He also made a number of recordings, often with Hudson "Tampa Red" Whittaker. Although a professing Christian, he kept a foot in both camps, writing and recording secular songs, often with suggestive lyrics, while also dabbling in Gospel music. His first Gospel song was "If You See My Saviour, Tell Him That You Saw Me."

Eventually, after struggling with nervous breakdown, God convicted him, and he decided to devote his life solely to the Gospel. A key event in this process was the decision to allow him to perform his songs and sell his music at the National Baptist Convention (Negroes) in 1930. His success there guaranteed a place for his music in church repertoires throughout the United States.

Dorsey went on to open the first Black Gospel music publishing company, Dorsey House of Music. He also founded his own gospel choir and was a founder and first president of the National Convention of Gospel Choirs and Choruses.

In 1932, however, tragedy struck with the death of his first wife in childbirth. Out of the pain of this experience, Dorsey wrote one of the most beautiful Christian songs of all time – "Precious Lord Take My Hand." This song was sung four times at the 1935 National Baptist Convention.

A number of singers moved to Chicago and joined Dorsey's Pilgrim Baptist Church. Among them were Theodore Frye, Sallie Martin, Roberta Martin and Mahalia Jackson. Sallie Martin and Roberta Martin (no relation) later went on to form their own singing groups.

Dorsey toured between 1932 and 1944, performing concerts with the above singers, and others that he had trained. The country was gradually emerging from the Great Depression, so admission to "Evenings with Dorsey" was kept

---

[56] Cusic, *op. cit.*, p. 163.

as low as possible. The singers were "demonstrators." They would demonstrate a song, and then sell the sheet music for five cents a copy. This was a shrewd business move, since people could afford to buy individual songs, whereas they couldn't afford whole song books, which had been the practice of publishers up till then.

Another very famous song, written in 1937 for Mahalia Jackson, came to Dorsey when he was travelling on a train through a beautiful valley. It was the late 1930s, and war was threatening in Europe. As Dorsey looked on the scene, he wondered why mankind could not live in peace like the animals in the field. Out of this experience came "Peace in the Valley."

In 1941, Dorsey married Kathryn Mosley, and the couple had a son and a daughter.

Thomas Dorsey died at the age of 93. He was the first African-American elected to the Nashville Songwriters' Hall of Fame and the Gospel Music Association's Living Hall of Fame.

The Story of "Precious Lord"

"Back in 1932 I was 32 years old and a fairly new husband. My wife, Nettie and I were living in a little apartment on Chicago's Southside. One hot August afternoon I had to go to St. Louis, where I was to be the featured soloist at a large revival meeting. I didn't want to go. Nettie was in the last month of pregnancy with our first child. But a lot of people were expecting me in St. Louis. . . .."

In the steaming St. Louis heat, the crowd called on me to sing again and again. When I finally sat down, a messenger boy ran up with a Western Union telegram. I ripped open the envelope. Pasted on the yellow sheet were the words: YOUR WIFE JUST DIED. . . .

"When I got back, I learned that Nettie had given birth to a boy. I swung between grief and joy. Yet that night, the baby died. I buried Nettie and our little boy together, in the same casket. Then I fell apart. For days I closeted myself. I felt that God had done me an injustice. I didn't want to serve Him anymore or write gospel songs. I just wanted to go back to that jazz world I once knew so well. . .

"But still I was lost in grief. Everyone was kind to me, especially a friend, Professor Frye, who seemed to know what I needed. On the following Saturday evening he took me up to Malone's Poro College, a neighborhood music school. It was quiet; the late evening sun crept through the curtained windows. I sat down at the piano, and my hands began to browse over the keys."

The tune he played was an old hymn – "Must Jesus Bear the Cross Alone." As he played with the tune, the words came to him.

Precious Lord, take my hand,
Lead me on, let me stand
I am tired, I am weak, I am worn;
Through the storm, through the night,
Lead me on to the light:
Take my hand, precious Lord,
Lead me home.

"Precious Lord" was later recorded by many famous singers, including Elvis Presley, Mahalia Jackson, Roy Rogers, and Tennessee Ernie Ford. It was the favourite song of Martin Luther King Jr., and was sung at the rally in Memphis the night before he was assassinated. President Lyndon B. Johnson requested that "Precious Lord" be sung at his funeral.

Mahalia Jackson (1911 – 1972)

Mahalia Jackson was born in New Orleans. She began her singing career at the local Mount Moriah Baptist Church, and at 12 years old, she was baptised in the Mississippi River.

After moving to Chicago, she sang in the Greater Salem Baptist Church Choir and joined

Mahalia Jackson

the Johnson Gospel Singers, one of the earliest professional Black Gospel groups. Thomas Dorsey became her mentor and voice trainer, and she toured with him for many years. She made "Precious Lord" her theme song.

While she made some recordings in the 1930s, Jackson's first major success came in 1947, with the song "Move on up a Little Higher." It sold millions of copies and became the highest selling Gospel single in history. Radio and television appearances and tours followed. On October 4, 1950, she performed for the first time in New York's Carnegie Hall. Jackson also had a successful 1952 European tour, and she was especially popular in France and Norway. In 1954 she was given her own weekly radio programme, broadcast by the CBS network. This was the only Gospel programme in the United States at the time.

Jackson also played a major role in the Civil Rights movement of the late 1950s and 1960s, beginning with the Montgomery Bus Boycott in 1956 and culminating with the March on Washington, D.C. in 1963. Jackson performed "I Been 'Buked and I Been Scorned," before King gave his famous "I Have a Dream" speech. Five years later she would perform "Precious Lord" at Dr. King's funeral.

By the time of her death, in 1972, Jackson was known internationally as the "Queen of Gospel Songs." In fact, Gospel songs were the only songs she would sing. On a number of occasions, she was pressured to sing other types of secular songs, but she would not do so. She said, "I sing God's music because it makes me feel free, it gives me hope. With the blues, when you finish, you still have the blues."

"If You See My Saviour, Tell Him You Saw Me" – try and listen to Thomas Dorsey and Sallie Martin singing this song

"It's A Highway to Heaven"

"Peace in the Valley"

"Precious Lord" – listen to Mahalia Jackson singing this song

Listen to Roberta Martin putting a Black Gospel spin on "What a Friend We Have in Jesus."

Doris Akers (1923 – 1995)

Doris Akers began playing the piano at age six. She wrote her first song, "Keep the Fires Burning in Me," when she was ten. After moving to Los Angeles in 1945, Akers joined the Sallie Martin Singers, and later formed her own group.

She is probably best known for composing the song "Sweet, Sweet Spirit," but she was also a recording artist, music arranger and choir director. She formed the Sky Pilot Choir and co-wrote "Lord Don't Move the Mountain" with her long-time friend, Mahalia Jackson. Later in life, she appeared in a number of Bill Gaither's concerts and television productions. She earned the affectionate title of "Miss Gospel Music."

 "Sweet, Sweet Spirit"

Audrey Mieir (1916 – 1996)

Audrey Mieir wrote about 1,000 songs, mostly Gospel. The most famous of these was "His Name Is Wonderful." Mieir was an ordained minister and a gifted musician. She worked closely with Doris Akers, and helped a young Andrae Crouch gain fame. She founded the internationally famous Harmony Chorus, and established two orphanages in Korea.

Shortly before her death at the age of 80, Mieir said, "'His Name is Wonderful' will outlive the chubby human hands chosen to write a few black notes on five lines and four spaces. But it will never outlive the Father who glories in His Son's name and who glories in our praise."[57]

 "His Name Is Wonderful"

---

[57]   Lucy Neeley Adams, "His Name Is Wonderful," <http://www.crosswalk.com/church/worship/his-name-is-wonderful-11562301.html>.

The Golden Age of Black Gospel

In the years 1940 to 1970, it is estimated that about five million African-Americans migrated from the southern states of the USA to the cities of the northern and western states, in what has become known as a Great Migration. During this same time period, Black Gospel experienced its Golden Age.

As African-Americans became more affluent, and black music became more acceptable to white audiences, there was a growing demand for Black Gospel performers, from both recording studios and radio stations. Radio stations had multiplied in number, but with the advent of television, radio had to find new programming to replace the network programmes that had moved to the new media.

While Black Gospel quartets continued to be popular, African-Americans also featured prominently in choirs and vocal groups. The first professional black gospel choir was called Wings over Jordan. It was founded in 1935 by Glenn T. Settle, a minister of the Gethsemane Baptist Church in Cleveland. From 1937, the music group was heard weekly in the Negro Hour program at the WGAR station that was connected to CBS Radio. Another choir, the St. Paul Baptist Church Choir of Los Angeles, directed by James Earl Hines, used hand clapping, solo spots, polyphony and antiphonal singing, which are all typical of gospel choirs now.

The revivalist preacher, A. A. Allen, was one who featured racially integrated choirs, long before this was common practice elsewhere in the southern states. Television shows originated from his headquarters in "Miracle Valley," Arizona, during the 1950s.

Listen to original recordings of the Wings over Jordan Choir and the St. Paul Baptist Church Choir of Los Angeles

"God's Not Dead," featuring Gene Martin and A. A. Allen. Note the racially integrated choir.

Civil Rights

Mahalia Jackson's involvement in the Civil Rights movement has already been noted. Another African-American Civil Rights campaigner was Fanny Lou Hamer. The youngest of 20 children, Hamer was instrumental in organising Mississippi's Freedom Summer, launched in June 1964 to attempt to register as many African-American voters as possible in Mississippi, which had historically excluded most blacks from voting. Later, Hamer became the vice-chair of the Mississippi Freedom Democratic Party.

Hamer frequently encouraged others by singing black Gospel songs, such as "Go Tell It on the Mountain," and "This Little Light of Mine." She saw the struggle for racial equality as a spiritual one, and frequently quoted Ephesians 6:11-12.

[11] Put on the whole armour of God, that ye may be able to stand against the wiles of the devil.

[12] For we wrestle not against flesh and blood, but against principalities, against powers, against the rulers of the darkness of this world, against spiritual wickedness in high places.

Her struggle was not an easy one. While having a tumour removed in 1961, she was forcibly sterilised as part of Mississippi's plan to reduce the number of poor blacks in the state. Then in 1963, she and a group of activists were arrested on false charges and beaten while in police custody. It took some time for her to recover from the physical and psychological abuse.

Fanny Lou Hamer

Despite mistreatment, her most famous quote was "I've been sick and tired for so long that I'm sick and tired of being sick and tired!"

 "Go Tell It On the Mountain," Fanny Lou Hamer

The Transition to Urban/Contemporary Gospel

During the 1970s, arguably the most important individual in traditional Black Gospel was James Cleveland. Born in 1931 in Chicago, he was a boy soprano in the church where Thomas Dorsey was minister of music. Later, he founded the Gospel Music Workshop, which provided help and instruction for Black Gospel musicians and singers.

Cleveland's sound was rough and raw – in the traditional Black Gospel style. However, he saw that black singers were gradually moving closer to the smooth, polished performance of whites, while the whites were taking on board aspects of black singing. "Somewhere in the middle of the road we're bound to run into one another," he stated.

The singer who bridged the gap between black and white audiences was Andrae Crouch.

Andrae Crouch (1942 – 2015)

Andrae Crouch

Andrae Crouch and his twin sister, Sandra, as well as an older brother Benjamin, were born in Los Angeles. Their father ran a dry cleaning business and did some street preaching, before becoming pastor of a small church at Val Verde. Here, Crouch developed his piano playing skill, which was largely self-taught. He also wrote his first song "The Blood Will Never Lose its Power" at the age of 14. He threw it in rubbish bin, but his sister rescued it, and it later became a Gospel classic.

After his father became pastor of the fledgling Christ Memorial Church of God in Christ at Pacoima, Crouch formed his first group, the COGICS (Church of God in Christ Singers). He also worked with David Wilkerson's Teen Challenge helping alcoholics and drug addicts. God cured him of stuttering, but he had a life-long battle with dyslexia.

In 1965, he formed the group Andrae Crouch and the Disciples. At the urging of composer Ralph Carmichael, he began to record his compositions on Carmichael's Light label. He also published his songs through Manna Music Publishing, which Tim Spencer (1908 – 1974) had founded in 1955. Spencer was a converted cowboy and former member of The Sons of The Pioneers.[58]

In 1975, Andrae Crouch and the Disciples became the first Gospel group to perform to sell-out crowds at Carnegie Hall. The group was also the first of its kind to perform at the Sydney Opera House, in Australia, and the Royal Albert Hall in London. They toured many countries of the world. Crouch's most popular songs from this period include "Jesus Is the Answer," "Take Me Back," "Through It All," "Bless His Holy Name," and "My Tribute."

The group disbanded in 1979, and Crouch went on to perform solo. In the early 1990s, following the death of his father, he and his sister Sandra became co-pastors of the church at Pacoima. He died following a heart attack in 2015.

Andrae Crouch is widely recognised as the first Black Gospel artist to appeal to both religious and secular audiences across multiracial lines. "Crouch was an innovator, a path-finder, a precursor in an industry noted for its conservative . . . approach to popular music. He combined gospel and rock, flavored it with jazz and calypso as the mood struck him and the song called for it."[59]

Select from the following Andrae Crouch songs.

"The Blood Will Never Lose Its Power"

"Jesus Is the Answer"

"Take Me Back"

"Through It All"

"Bless His Holy Name"

"My Tribute"

---

[58] The Sons of the Pioneers is a cowboy singing group. It was founded in 1933 by Tim Spencer, Bob Nolan and Roy Rogers.

[59] Robert Darden, "Remembering Andrae Crouch, Dead at 72," *Christianity Today*, January 8, 2015, <http://www.christianitytoday.com/ct/2015/january-web-only/remembering-andrae-crouch-dead-at-72.html>

Urban/Contemporary Gospel

Since the 1960s, there has been a great mingling and mixing of modern Christian music genres; so much so that it is sometimes hard to tell where one ends and another begins. For the sake of simplicity, we will distinguish between Urban/ Contemporary Gospel Music and Contemporary Christian Music (CCM).

Urban/Contemporary Gospel Music has its roots in Black Gospel. We have traced its origins and some of its history in previous pages. Contemporary Christian Music, on the other hand, owes its origins primarily to the Jesus Movement of the late 1960s. We will consider this in later chapters. While Gospel today is primarily black, and CCM white, there is considerable overlap, as evidenced in the life and music of Andrae Crouch.

According to Dwight Buckner, "When blacks take gospel and add funk to it, it becomes contemporary gospel music. When whites take gospel and add to it, it is classified contemporary Christian."[60]

Robert Darden further explains that CCM is "exactly the same as what you hear on (commercial) radio except it's message music. It's lyric-driven, whereas with everything else on the radio, the sound is No. 1." Urban/Contemporary Gospel, however, is a separate art form. "It has a series of rigid, unwritten rules: call and response, it almost always has a choir, it's open-ended, like the riffs [short repeated phrases] in pop music that are designed to reach an emotional peak."[61]

Not all artists agree with the racial distinction. Famous Gospel performer, CeCe Winans, states that "You can have contemporary music and it shouldn't be black or white. Music doesn't carry a color. The color issue is something that should be totally dissolved, and just go on the style of music, if you're going to categorize."[62]

---

[60] Jon Bream, "Divided Loyalties: Charts Split Gospel Music into Separate Camps," *Minneapolis-St. Paul Star Tribune*, October 27, 1991. <http://articles.chicagotribune.com/1991-10-27/entertainment/9104060840_1_gospel-music-billboard-two-charts>

[61] *Ibid.*

[62] *Ibid.*

As an example of Urban/Contemporary Gospel, listen to a song by Kirk Franklin and his choir, The Family.

"Oh Happy Day"

The hymn "Oh Happy Day" was originally written by Philip Doddridge, an eighteenth century dissenting clergyman. It was given a new tune and a chorus in the mid-nineteenth century by Edward D. Rimbault.

In 1968, the Edwin Hawkins Singers released their version of the song. Hawkins (born 1943) is one of the originators of the Urban/Contemporary Gospel sound. His gospel group was formed in 1967 in the Ephesian Church of God in Christ (COGIC) in Berkeley, California. After its release, the song reached number 4 on the US hit parade and number 2 in the UK. Note the use of call and response and short riffs. Some versions of the song also feature a choir.

Edwin Hawkins Singers, 1970

Try and sing the original "Oh Happy Day" from http://cyberhymnal.org/htm/o/h/ohappday.htm or http://www.hymnary.org/text/o_happy_day_that_fixed_my_choice

Listen to "Oh Happy Day" from Edwin Hawkins

Rap

Rap is a musical style where rhythmic and/or rhyming words are chanted (or "rapped") to a musical accompaniment.[63] Christian rap is a sub-genre of Urban/Contemporary Gospel. It originated amongst African-Americans in New York City in the 1970s.

The first explicitly Christian rap recording was made by McSweet (Pete Harrison) in 1982. The track was entitled "Jesus Christ (The Gospel Beat)." The first full-length, Christian rap album, *Bible Break*, by Oklahoma artist Stephen Wiley, was made in 1985. Prominent Christian rappers include tobyMac (Toby McKeehan), Lecrae and dc Talk.

Some conservative Christian commentators have criticised Christian rap because of its emphasis upon rhythm at the expense of melody, and because of rap music's association with violence, hatred, and sexuality.[64]

---

[63] Hip hop and rap are often said to be synonymous, however the Merriam-Webster Dictionary defines hip hop as "the stylized rhythmic music that commonly accompanies rap."

[64] See, for example, Scott Aniol, "Can Rap Be Christian? Evaluating Hip Hop," *Religious Affections Ministries*, October 9, 2009. <http://religiousaffections.org/articles/articles-on-music/can-rap-be-christian-evaluating-hip-hop>

You can listen to

"Jesus Christ (The Gospel Beat)" (McSweet)

"Bible Break" (Stephen Wiley)

You can watch the six episodes of the BBC documentary *The History of Gospel Music* on YouTube. Each episode is about 14 minutes long.

CHAPTER ELEVEN

SOUTHERN GOSPEL

Origins

Southern (white) Gospel grew out of the Second Great Awakening. This was a rural revival, largely associated with the southern states of the USA. As we have already seen, the songs associated with this Awakening were usually easy to learn, with repeating choruses. They often grew out of folk tradition. Both black and white Gospel music was strongly influenced by these rural revivals of the early 1800s. The simplicity of the songs solved the problem of lack of musical literacy, but this problem had already been tackled in a different way.

The singing school movement that began in New England in the 1720s (actually before then in England) aimed to help congregations sing from songbooks. Later, the singing schools became more strongly associated with the southern states, and became a key ingredient of Southern Gospel.

A typical singing school – called a "Normal" - would last for up to ten days, with intensive practice in sight reading, pitch and harmony. It usually wound up with a concert, in which the students demonstrated what they had learned.

An important ingredient of the singing school movement, from the late 1700s, was the use of shaped-note music. This was an attempt to visualise pitch using different shaped notes – round, rectangle, triangle and diamond. The most common was the four-note system, which used only the solfège syllables fa, sol, la and mi. The notes of a C major scale would be notated and sung as follows.

fa   sol   la   fa   sol   la   mi   fa

Later a seven-note system was developed by Jesse B. Aikin (there are other seven-note systems in use).

do   re   mi   fa   so   la   ti   do

Many music books were published using the shaped-note system. Some of these are still in print today, for example *Sacred Harp*. Shaped note singing was essentially a southern rural phenomenon. It was rejected by educated musicians from the cities of the northern USA.

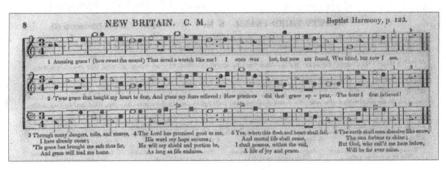

Amazing Grace in the 7-note system as used in a Baptist church hymnal.

Singing schools were an ideal method for selling songbooks. The singing school teacher was often a salesman working for one of the shaped-note publishing companies.

On a larger scale, singing conventions, which were held annually, also showcased new songs. There was some reaction to conventions from the established churches, who felt that they were "ungodly." However, the Holiness and Pentecostal people were not biased against the singing, nor were they biased against the use of instruments, especially "folk" instruments like the guitar.

Southern Gospel Quartets

In 1910, a publisher named James D. Vaughan hit upon another way of publicising songs – the touring quartet. The quartet was made up of bass, baritone, tenor and lead singers. Thus began a shift in Gospel publishing away from church congregations to an audience watching a performance.

To young Southern farm boys, singing school teachers and the members of travelling quartets were people to be respected and admired. They offered a glittering future for those who wanted to escape from the drudgery of farm life and make a future for themselves.

 Listen to the Vaughan Quartet

Shaped-note singing is still alive and well today, as part of the Southern Gospel heritage. There are many examples of shaped-note singing on YouTube.

In the years before World War Two, Southern Gospel quartets had a major advantage over Black Gospel quartets in that they were welcomed by radio stations whereas blacks were not. Especially during the difficult days of the Depression of the 1930s, Black Gospel quartets relied on recordings and personal appearances, but the future was in radio.

Not that the Depression years were easy for Southern Gospel quartets either. Whereas Country music singers could charge admission to their concerts, Gospel groups could not. They had to rely on freewill offerings, which were not much during the 1930s.

Many traditional churches regarded Gospel music as "entertainment," which could lead serious-minded Christians astray. Even the radio was seen as an enemy. Travelling quartets were criticised for lack of spiritual depth in their songs and performances. Those in Gospel music countered, however, that singing Gospel music was just as pleasing to God as preaching and prayer.[65]

Some Southern Gospel Composers

Janie West Metzgar

Janie West and her brother, Archie, were left in baskets on the step of Buckner's Baptist Orphanage, in Dallas, Texas. The note on Janie's basket read "Janie, baby girl." The staff of the orphanage raised her, giving her the name West, because she had been found on the west side of the chapel.

She suffered from leukaemia at an early age, and even when the disease was in remission, much of her life was spent in pain and suffering. Despite her illness, she earned a degree at Bayor University, Waco, Texas, and became an English teacher. She married William Metzgar and had five children.

Metzgar was an Assemblies of God pastor, and he also worked as tent manager for the revivalist Jack Coe. His church became a focal point for gospel singing. The Oak Ridge Boys, the Gatlins, the Statler Brothers, the Blackwood Brothers and other gospel groups made regular appearances at the church along with a host of very famous evangelists.

---

[65]   Cusic, *op. cit.*, p. 172

William and Janie Metzgar

Janie started writing songs at the age of 12. Her first songs were published as sheet music in the early 1920s. Two of her most famous songs were "Jesus Breaks Every Fetter" (1927) and "Where the Roses Never Fade" (1929). The latter song was written in collaboration with one of her sons, Robert Metzgar, who composed the music.

As well as working with the founder of Youth with a Mission, Loren Cunningham, Robert also worked as an Assemblies of God missionary on a number of fields in Central and South America, Africa and Asia. He was associated with the ministry of Teen Challenge founder, David Wilkerson. He currently works as a music producer.

Janie West Metzgar took part in many Civil Rights marches. She believed that racial discrimination was a sin, and these sentiments were reflected in her songs. She also became well known as an anti-Vietnam War protester, often carrying the sign "Jesus died too."

She died on August 16, 1977, after a long battle with breast cancer. Coincidentally, Elvis Presley died on the same day.

"Where the Roses Never Fade"
"Jesus Breaks Every Fetter"

Albert Brumley

Albert E. Brumley (1905 – 1977)

Albert Brumley was born in Oklahoma when it was still Indian Territory. His parents were sharecroppers, and he spent much of his early life chopping and picking cotton on his family's farm. He heard that the head of the Hartford Musical Institute, **Eugene Bartlett (1883 – 1941)**, sometimes offered free tuition to students who couldn't afford the fees.

Bartlett had started as a singing school teacher. In 1918, he founded the Hartford Music Company and published many shaped-note songbooks featuring his own and other people's work. In 1939, two years before his death, he wrote the famous song, "Victory in Jesus," which has regained popularity in evangelical churches since the 1960s.

 "Victory in Jesus"

After paying 50 cents for a bus ride to Hartford, Albert Brumley was left with $2.50. Bartlett not only agreed to give him free tuition, but took him into his own home and gave him free room and board.

Brumley taught singing schools and appeared in many singing conventions. He married Goldie Schell in 1931. She was a great help to him, as he was totally disorganised, and frequently lost songs that he had jotted down on pieces of paper. He wrote both words and music. His wife helped him and critiqued his songs, but she never wrote any herself.

By the early 1940s, Brumley was earning $200 a month as a songwriter for the Stamp-Baxter Music Company in Dallas, Texas. In 1943, he formed his own publishing company, Albert E. Brumley and Sons, and in 1948, he bought the Hartford Music Company.

Brumley wrote over 700 songs. In a study of gospel music the Smithsonian Institution wrote that he was the "greatest white gospel songwriter before World War II."

 "Turn Your Radio On"
"I'll Fly Away"
"He Set Me Free"

Virgil O. Stamps

Virgil O. Stamps (1892 – 1940)

As a young person, Stamps worked in his father's sawmill and used all the money he earned to buy Gospel songbooks. He started his career as a singing school teacher, and then went on to work for the James D. Vaughan Music Company between 1914 and 1924. After that he formed the V. O. Stamps Music Company, and in 1927, he joined with J. R. Baxter to form the Stamps-Baxter Music Company in Dallas, Texas.

The songbooks that they published were used in church singing events, called "conventions," as well as at other church events. Gospel songs first published by Stamps-Baxter include "Just a Little Talk with Jesus," "Precious Memories," "If We Never Meet Again" and "Victory in Jesus."

Another major part of the corporation was its sponsorship of gospel quartets who sang the company's music in churches throughout the southern United States. The Frank Stamps Quartet (named after V. O's brother) pioneered the use of a separate pianist, or "fifth man."

Stamps wrote about 1,500 Gospel songs, including, possibly, the music for one version of "Oh When the Saints Go Marching In." **Luther G. Presley (1887 – 1974)** wrote the lyrics.[66]

"The Saints" already existed as a traditional song associated with jazz funerals in New Orleans. Often a slow version would be played on the way to the cemetery and a fast version on the way back. The musicians at Preservation Hall in New Orleans got so tired of playing it that the sign announcing the fee schedule ran $1 for standard requests, $2 for unusual requests, and $5 for "The Saints." (By 2004 the price had gone up to $10.)

"Oh When the Saints Go Marching In" has been used as the theme song for a number of sports teams, in the USA and Britain. In Australia, it is used by St. George Illawarra Dragons (NRL) and St Kilda Football Club ("The Saints") (AFL).

"Oh When the Saints Go Marching In" - try and listen to a version that begins "I am just a weary pilgrim," or "I am just a lonesome trav'ler."

"When All of God's Singers Get Home" – this song was also composed by Presley and Stamps.

In the period 1926 to 1930, recording companies travelled the country, particularly in the South, doing "field recordings" of promising talent. Charles Wolfe states that between 1925 and 1931, Columbia released 11 million records on its 15000-D label. Fifteen percent of these were gospel releases.[67]

---

[66]   Gregory H. Jacks, "I Want to Be in That Number: A Song Profile of 'When the Saints Go Marching In'," *Syracuse University Honors Program Capstone Project*, Paper 817, 2015, p. 10. <http://surface.syr.edu/cgi/viewcontent.cgi?article=1818&context=honors_capstone> Jacks claims that there were other versions of the song long before Stamps and Presley were supposed to have written it, in 1937.

[67]   Charles Wolfe, "Columbia Records and Old-Time Music," *JEMF Quarterly*, pp. 118-125, 144.

Southern Gospel after World War Two

Because there were large areas of vacant land in the South, many of the Army's training camps were established there during World War Two. As a result, about six million non-Southerners were exposed to Southern Gospel music for the first time. In addition, many Southern boys travelled far and wide with the armed forces, taking their love of Gospel singing with them. After the war, the demand for Gospel quartets led to a national awareness of Southern Gospel music.

Before the war, publishing companies, such as the Vaughan Music Company and the Stamps-Baxter Company, had depended on touring quartets to sell the music they were publishing. Now, the power of these companies declined as groups became more independent, and, in some cases, wrote their own songs.

After World War Two, the growth of both Black and Southern Gospel music was closely associated with Pentecostalism. This was because Pentecostals were much more ready to accept new styles of music than were mainline churches. They believed that popular music with Christian lyrics could be a powerful tool to reach people who would not normally accept traditional church services.

A booming US economy also helped the development of new music. However, some Gospel groups that sang both secular and Gospel songs found themselves pressured to choose one or the other. Many Christians felt strongly that secular "pop" songs were sinful, and that Christians who sung them were selling out to the Devil. Even today, there is a stigma attached to Gospel singers who "cross-over" to sing secular music. Some justify it by claiming that it is just entertainment. But the question then arises as to whether Gospel songs should ever just be about entertainment.

The rural singing conventions began to die out in the face of radio and TV, as did the touring Gospel groups. As they died, the shaped-note publishing business all but died too. As the old died, it was replaced with the new technology – sound systems, tape recorders, and television.

New groups that were formed at this time to exploit the new mass media included the Blue Ridge Quartet and the Homeland Harmony Quartet.

Listen to Leroy Abernathy and the Homeland Harmony Quartet singing "A Wonderful Time up There" ("Gospel Boogie").

The 1948 recording of Leroy Abernathy and the Homeland Harmony Quartet singing "A Wonderful Time up There" caused an uproar. A critic (from one of the singing convention publishers) stated "Why should people who love the Lord and clean Christian society have to listen to the music of the 'juke box' to find a medium of expression toward God? . . . Why should a so-called Christian audience go crazy over an all-night jamboree which is so often opened with a prayer but is thereafter carried on as if there were no God?"[68]

There was some truth in the accusation. Many Southern Gospel singers put an emphasis on entertainment, rather than "ministry," and in some cases, they were not really true believers, but rather boys who had been raised in Christian homes and enjoyed singing. However, Christians who received a heavy dose of preaching in their churches on Sunday, and on week-days too, did not necessarily want the same thing in the Gospel concerts. They wanted safe, wholesome family fun, and the Gospel concerts provided it. Nevertheless, tension remained between ministry and entertainment.

Southern Gospel "Greats"

On 5 November 1948, **Wally Fowler** held the first "All-Night Sing" from the Ryman Auditorium, home of the Grand Ole Opry in Nashville. All-night shows soon spread to other towns and cities throughout the South. Fowler's group became known as the **Oak Ridge Quartet**. It was named after the town in Tennessee where much of the secret work had been done to develop the atomic bombs, dropped on Hiroshima and Nagasaki at the end of the War. In the 1960s, the quartet changed its name to the Oak Ridge Boys. Later in the 1970s, they

---

[68] Charles K. Wolfe, "'Gospel Boogie': White Southern Gospel Music in Transition, 1945-55," <http://nativeground.com/gospel-boogie-white-southern-gospel-music-transition-1945-55-charles-wolfe/>.

"crossed over" to become a country music band and effectively lost the support of the Southern Gospel community.

 Listen to the Oak Ridge Quartet

Another very influential group was the **Statesmen Quartet**, formed in 1948 by 21-year old pianist, **Hovie Lister (1926 – 2001).**

Hovie Lister and the Statesmen Quartet. Seated Jack Toney
(lead), Hovie Lister (piano) and Wallace Nelms (tenor);
standing Doug Young (bass) and Rick Fair (baritone).

Hovie Lister was born in Greenville, South Carolina. He leaned to play the piano at a young age, and, while still a teenager, he was asked to accompany evangelist Mordecai Ham and his music director, C. Austin Miles, in a city-wide revival in his home town.

Lister attended the Stamps-Baxter School of Music in Dallas, in 1942. He subsequently played for a number of Gospel groups before forming the Statesmen

Quartet in 1948. In his autobiography, Bill Gaither recalls hearing Lister play at one of Wally Fowler's "All-Night Sings." "He was bouncing all over the piano stool and pulling at his pant legs, revealing his trademark red socks, when his fingers weren't flying up and down the keyboard."[69]

An ordained Southern Baptist preacher, Lister also took seriously his ministerial responsibilities, pastoring the Mount Zion Baptist Church in Cobb County, Georgia.

The original lead singer for the Statesmen Quartet was **Mosie Lister (1921 – 2015)** (no relation). When he left the quartet, he retired from singing and devoted himself to song writing and publishing. His songs include "Where No One Stands Alone," "Then I Met the Master" and "How Long Has It Been?"

Jake Hess (1927 – 2004) became the lead singer for the Statesmen between 1948 and 1963. He then formed his own group, **The Imperials**. They were not immediately accepted because of their innovative use of electric guitars and drums. However, they went on to become pioneers in Contemporary Christian Music, and backed Elvis Presley from 1966 to 1971. Hess was also an ordained Baptist minister.

 Listen to Hovie Lister and the Statesmen Quartet

 Listen to Jake Hess and the Imperials

 "Where No Man Stands Alone"
"How Long Has It Been?"

The family group known as **The Speers** was founded in 1921 by George Thomas ("Dad") Speer (d. 1966) and his wife Lena ("Mom") Speer (d. 1967). Four children joined – Brock, Rosa Nell, Mary Tom and Ben.

Dad Speer had been born to farming parents. He entered third grade at age 23 and finished in Grade 7 at age 27. While he farmed and worked as a singing school teacher, he also attended a number of "all-day singings." These served as

---

[69] Bill Gaither, *It's More than Music*, Warner Faith, 2003, p. 35.

a social gathering, church picnic and entertainment for poor rural Southerners. These events grew larger and more organised and eventually became state conventions that attracted thousands of people.

In the early 1940s, The Speers moved to Montgomery, Alabama, where they had a regular radio programme advertising Stamps-Baxter songbooks. Later they went into television. In the years that followed, the group went through many configurations until it was officially retired at the 1998 National Quartet Convention.

Brock spent almost his entire life singing with The Speers. He was also a licensed minister, and heavily involved with the Gospel Music Association. His brother Ben revived the Stamps-Baxter School of Music in 1988, and served as music director for the Gaither Homecoming videos, in which he and his two sisters also appeared.

 Listen to a recording of The Speers

Another family group was the **Blackwood Brothers**. Three brothers Roy, Doyle and James joined with Roy's 13-year-old son R. W. Blackwood to form the quartet in 1934. The group was innovative in its use of advertising. When they arrived at a location they would drive around in a car with powerful loud speakers that could cover a mile radius attached to the roof promoting their evening concert.

The group reorganised several times. Following a plane crash in 1954, which claimed the lives of R. W. and the current bass singer, Bill Lyles, Cecil Blackwood (R. W's younger brother) was brought in to sing baritone, while J. D. Sumner became the new bass.

In the mid-1950s the quartet became the first to start travelling in a customized tour bus. Elvis Presley later copied this idea.

In 1957, James, Cecil and J. D. Sumner founded the National Quartet Convention in Memphis, Tennessee.

Listen to the Blackwood Brothers

J. D. Sumner (1924 – 1998) is credited with having one of the lowest singing voices in the world. His vocal range extended below the lowest playable note on the piano, reaching the note G0. He sang with the Blackwood Brothers from 1954 to 1965. After that, he sang with the **Stamps Quartet**, which he renamed J. D. Sumner & The Stamps.

 Listen to J.D. Sumner singing

Elvis Presley loved Sumner's singing, and in 1971 he hired Sumner & The Stamps as his back-up singers. The group toured and recorded with Presley from November 1971 until Presley's death in 1977.

Another member of the group was J.D's nephew, **Donnie Sumner**. Even although he was brought up as a Christian, Donnie could not escape the strong temptations of the show business circuit. By 1976, his life was in ruins and he was a helpless drug addict.

As he stood on the balcony of a 28-storey apartment block and considered ending his life, he cried out to God and God met him in a miraculous way and turned his life around. A few days later, he left Presley's group. When he told Presley that he was leaving, the singer replied, "I'm proud of you. I wish I could do that. I'd love to start over, and do and be what I like, but I can't....I've just got to keep on being Elvis."[70] A year later, Presley was dead.

 You can read Donnie Sumner's testimony, or listen to it at https://www. youtube.com/watch?v=9HxDr4xNO4w

---

[70] "On the Road with Elvis," Donnie Sumner, <http://www.donniesumner.com/voice_testimony.asp>.

George Younce (1930 – 2005) was involved in a number of Southern Gospel groups before he joined the **Cathedral Quartet** as bass singer in 1964, along with his friend, Glen Payne. They toured the world for 35 years, performing at Billy Graham Crusades, on Gaither Homecoming videos, and at many other venues, such as Carnegie Hall and Radio City Music Hall.

In 1990, **Ernie Haase (b. 1964)** became tenor singer for the group. Haase married Younce's third daughter, Lisa, and when the Cathedral Quartet disbanded in 1999, following the death of Glen Payne, Haase formed a new group called **Ernie Haase and Signature Sound.**

 Listen to George Younce and the Cathedral Quartet

 Listen to Ernie Haase and Signature Sound

The Kingsmen Quartet is a prestigious Southern Gospel group that formed in 1956.

 Listen to the Kingsmen Quartet singing "When God Ran"

The Happy Goodman Family started singing together in the 1940s, with various combinations of the eight Goodman children. Howard's wife, Vestal, also joined the group. She was nine years his junior. Together they had a son, Rick, and a daughter Vicki. They pastored churches and sang to congregations across the USA.

During the 1960s and 1970s, The Goodmans were one of the first groups to use a live band. They also developed their classic "grab a note and hang on" endings. Howard's brother, Rusty, wrote most of their songs, while Howard was a virtuoso on the piano. Vestal

Vestal Goodman

151

was renowned for her elaborate hairdos and an omnipresent white handkerchief that she would wave at audiences. In the 1980s, Rusty and Sam Goodman, and Rusty's daughter, Tanya, wanted to move in a more contemporary direction, while Howard and Vestal wanted to retain the traditional sound. As a result of this difference, the Happy Goodmans only sang together once between 1984 and 1990.

In 1993, the Happy Goodman name was resurrected as a trio featuring Howard, Vestal and former band member Johnny Minnick.

In their later years, the Happy Goodmans were regular guests on the Gaither Homecoming events. Howard died in 2002 and Vestal in 2003.

 Listen to the Happy Goodman Family.

Russ Taff (born 1953) is the son of a fiery Pentecostal preacher and a musical mother. He has sung a variety of musical styles throughout his career including pop rock, traditional Southern Gospel, contemporary Country Music and rhythm and blues. Between 1977 and 1981, he was lead vocalist for The Imperials. He has also been a member of the Gaither Vocal Band, and occasionally tours with the Gaither Homecoming concerts. As a solo artist and songwriter, Taff is known for the 1980s anthem "We Will Stand."

 Listen as Bill Gaither interviews Russ Taff about his battle with doubt and depression. https://www.youtube.com/watch?v=QTYddNynmHU

 "We Will Stand," written by Taff and his wife Tori

Dottie Rambo (1934 - 2008) was one of the greats of Southern Gospel. Along with her husband, Buck, and daughter, Reba, she formed the award-winning Southern Gospel group known first as The Singing Rambos, and later as The Rambos. She wrote over 2,500 Gospel songs, including "Holy Spirit, Thou Art Welcome in This Place," "We Shall Behold Him," and "I Go to the Rock."

When she became a Christian, at the age of 12, her father gave her the option of giving up Christian music or leaving home. She chose the latter option. Her first group was a trio known as The Gospel Echoes.

Later, after her marriage to Buck, The Singing Rambos toured extensively, including a trip to Vietnam in 1967 to minister to American troops.

The 1980s and 90s were difficult times. In 1987, she suffered a ruptured disk, which left her partially disabled. After years of marital difficulties, Buck and Dottie divorced in 1994.

In 2002, she recorded her first solo album in 18 years. She followed this up with further concerts and recordings. However, she died as a result of injuries sustained in a bus accident in 2008.

 "Holy Spirit, Thou Art Welcome in This Place"
"We Shall Behold Him"
"I Go to the Rock"

The Gaithers

No study would be complete without considering Bill and Gloria Gaither, who have done more than any other couple to popularise Southern Gospel music over a long period of time. Although they have also been influential in promoting Contemporary Christian Music, as well as Urban/Contemporary Gospel, Southern Gospel has remained their first love.

Bill Gaither (born 1936) has spent all his life in the town of Alexandria, Indiana. He started his first group, known as the Bill Gaither Trio, in 1956. The trio initially included Bill, his sister Mary Ann, and his brother Danny.

Gaither trained as an English teacher and married fellow teacher, Gloria Sickal, in 1962. In 1964, Gloria took Mary Ann's place in the trio. Gaither resigned from teaching in 1967, so he could devote himself full time to Gospel music.

The Gaithers recorded their breakthrough song, "He Touched Me," in 1964. Since then, they have composed well over 700 songs, including the vastly popular "The King Is Coming," "Something Beautiful," "It Is Finished," "Jesus There's Something about That Name" and "Let's Just Praise the Lord."

The 1960s were years of massive social change, which will be dealt with in a later chapter. By the end of the decade, the Gaithers were dealing with many personal struggles. Bill was recovering from mononucleosis, the couple had been accused of profiting from their ministry, and the family had been devastated by Mary Ann's divorce. Gloria was expecting her third child, but the couple was worried about bringing another child into a world filled with racial tension, drug abuse and negative attitudes toward Christianity. After receiving prayer, they were filled with the assurance that God would take care of them. Inspired by the birth of a healthy son Benjamin (Benji) in 1970, the Gaithers wrote "Because He Lives." This has become one of the great classics of the Christian church.

Over the years, the composition of the Bill Gaither Trio changed many times, until it was superseded by the Gaither Vocal Band, in 1981. Although initially a quartet, the name did not imply numbers, and in 2009, the band was expanded to a quintet.

The singers who have had the longest association with the Gaither Vocal Band are Guy Penrod, Mark Lowry, Michael English, David Phelps and Wes Hampton.

The Gaither Vocal Band in 2009. (l to r) Michael English, Bill Gaither, Mark Lowry, David Phelps and Wes Hampton.

As well as being a baritone singer, Mark Lowry has delighted audiences as a comedian. Bill Gaither is often the (willing) butt of his jokes.

Much of Gaither's success is a result of his skills as an entrepreneur. The Gaither Music Company functions as a record company, retail store and recording studio, as well as in the areas of concert booking, television production, and copyright management.

Much of the Gaithers' early work was in the Contemporary Christian Music genre. A number of famous CCM stars, such as Michael W. Smith, Carman, Sandi Patty, Steve Green, Don Francisco and Amy Grant look upon Gaither as a mentor and father figure.

From the 1960s through to the 1980s, Southern Gospel music went through a low period. The advent of the Jesus Revolution and Contemporary Christian Music not only made Southern Gospel look old fashioned, it also removed a significant section of its fan base, especially amongst young people.

A new swing towards Southern Gospel, however, occurred with the establishment of the Gaither Homecoming in 1991. "Homecoming" is an American term that refers to the welcoming home of students and former residents. There are usually sports competitions, a parade, a dance and the crowning of a Homecoming King and Queen. In the church, a "homecoming" consists of special services to celebrate church heritage and welcome back former members or pastors.

The concept of the Gaither Homecoming was to welcome back Gospel singers, both past and present. The idea originated on 19 February 1991. Many of the Southern Gospel artists profiled on the preceding pages had just completed a recording session in Nashville, for an album called *Homecoming*. Afterwards, they stayed around, singing old favourites and swapping stories. This impromptu session was recorded on video and later published.

The success of this enterprise prompted a whole series of Homecoming videos and CDs. Several dozen singers would be brought together on a studio set. Long established singers would sit in the front row, with new and upcoming artists further back. Gaither would lead the whole group in several classics, and there would also be numbers performed by soloists and smaller groups, as well as interviews with the legends of Southern Gospel. By the mid-2000s, most of these legends had died, but they were being replaced by new talent, such as the

Nelons, the Martins and Jeff and Sheri Easter. There were also a few African-American groups singing Southern Gospel.

Don Cusic states that "Bill Gaither 'saved' Southern gospel by giving it national exposure and a new sense of pride and elevating it when the field was at its lowest point."[71]

In 1996, Homecoming concert tours were started, and later, cruises to Alaska and the Caribbean. It was on one of these cruises, in 2006, that the popular pianist, Anthony Burger, died from a massive heart attack while performing on stage. Burger was only 44 years old at the time.

There is a very large amount of material available for the Gaithers. Try and watch the Bill Gaither Trio, the Gaither Vocal Band, and one or more of the Gaither Homecoming videos. Try and listen to Guy Penrod, Mark Lowry, Michael English, David Phelps and Wes Hampton. You will also enjoy Mark Lowry's comedy routines, such as "Denominations," "Jesus on the Mainline," or "Comedy and TV Tunes" (there are many more).

You can sing or listen to Gaither songs such as:
"He Touched Me"
"The King is Coming"
"Jesus, I Heard You Have a Big House"
"Jesus There's Something about That Name"
"I Just Feel like Something Good is about to Happen"
"Let's Just Praise the Lord"
"It Is Finished"
"Something Beautiful"
"I Am a Promise"

Watch the BBC documentary on Southern Gospel (White Gospel) on YouTube

---

[71] Cusic, *op. cit.*, p.379.

CHAPTER TWELVE

MAINLINE GOSPEL AFTER WORLD WAR TWO

For most people, the 1950s was a decade of unheard of prosperity. The new "Baby Boomer" generation helped encourage sales of farm products and manufactured goods. A new world of consumerism opened up. The traditional values of thrift and saving were now discouraged. There was a rapid housing boom, and suburbs sprawled ever outwards from the cities. Aided by the increasing use of motor cars, shopping complexes and supermarkets began to appear. No one bothered about pollution or climate change – petrol was a few cents a litre.

Family, church and community remained the pillars of society during the prosperous years of the 1950s. In 1955, 33 percent of Australians claimed to be "regular churchgoers," and the membership of mainstream churches rose throughout the decade, to peak in the 1960s.

Women were encouraged to resume their role as wives and mothers after the war, although an increasing number entered the workforce. Fashions remained modest and conservative, with dresses well below the knee for women, and double-breasted suits, white shirts and short-back-and-sides haircuts the norm for men. The desire to make or *keep* the nation Christian was strongly maintained, and there was considerable investment of time and money in missions work and evangelism.

Although urban Gospel songs such as "Blessed Assurance," "To God Be the Glory," "Since Jesus Came into My Heart," "The Glory Song" and "It Is Well with My Soul" had been around for half a century, they were still resisted by some traditional mainstream churches. George Beverly Shea and Billy Graham did more than anyone to bring evangelical Gospel music into the mainstream.

Billy Graham (1918 - 2018)

William Franklin Graham Jnr. has been cred-ited with preaching to more people than any-one else in history. There was little indication of his future fame, however, when he was born on a dairy farm in Charlotte, North Carolina, the first of four children.

Billy Graham

He was brought up in a Christian family, and made a decision for Christ at the age of 16, when he attended some revival meetings run by evangelist Mordecai Ham. After high school, he enrolled in Bob Jones University, but did not like the rigid doctrine, so he transferred to Florida Bible Institute. In 1939, he was ordained as a Baptist minister.

In 1943, he enrolled at Wheaton College, Illinois. Here he met his future wife, Ruth Bell. Ruth was the daughter of missionaries, and had lived in China until the age of 17. The couple were married in 1943.

After briefly pastoring First Baptist Church in Western Springs, Illinois, Graham joined Youth for Christ. In 1947, he became president of Northwestern Bible College. In 1952, however, he resigned to concentrate on preaching.

His first major crusade, which brought him to the attention of the nation, took place in Los Angeles, in 1949.

A number of famous personalities were converted, including the 1936 5,000 metre Olympic star, Louis Zamperini, the underworld criminal Jim Vaus, and the radio cowboy Stuart Hamblen. Hamblen invited Graham on to his radio show, and newspaper magnate, William Randolph Hearst, told his editors to "puff Graham," (cover his meetings closely). As a result of this publicity, the Los Angeles Crusade was extended from three to eight weeks.

Graham and his associates formed the Billy Graham Evangelistic Association (BGEA) in 1950. It was founded on a series of ethical guidelines known as The

Modesto Manifesto. Graham also used mass media to spread the Gospel, beginning with radio and books, and progressing on to films and television. The popular magazine *Christianity Today* was also started by BGEA in 1955.

Until his retirement in 2005, Graham preached in over 400 crusades worldwide. He ministered in the Communist nations of Eastern Europe before the collapse of Communism there. He also ministered in China and North Korea. In 1959, crusades in Australia resulted in a nationwide revival.[72]

Although he has been criticised for being too liberal in theology and for not supporting a political party, Graham has consistently been rated one of the world's most respected and influential persons. He was a long-time supporter of the American Civil Rights movement, and has been a respected advisor to numerous Presidents, from Dwight Eisenhower through to George Bush.

In 1992, he was diagnosed with hydrocephalus, a disease similar to Parkinson's. He and Ruth retired to their home in Montreat, North Carolina, leaving their son, William Franklin Graham III to head up BGEA. Ruth passed away in 2007, leaving five children, 19 grandchildren and numerous great-grandchildren. Billy Graham died on 21 February 2018.

George Beverly Shea (1909 - 2013)

George Beverly Shea was born in Canada in February 1909, the fourth of eight children. He was the son of a minister. His name was originally just Beverly Shea; the "George" was added later on at the insistence of an advertising agency that felt listeners would be confused listening to a young man called "Beverly"!

Shea worked as a medical secretary for an insurance company and sang at functions and on the radio. In 1932, he wrote the music to "I'd Rather Have Jesus" from a poem by Mrs Rhea Miller. He also wrote both lyrics and music for "The Wonder of it All" in 1955.

---

[72] Documented by Stuart Piggin in his book *Evangelical Christianity in Australia - Spirit, Word and World*, Acorn Press, Brunswick East, 2012.

 **"I'd Rather Have Jesus"**

In 1939, Shea was offered a job at Moody Bible Institute radio station, WMBI. Billy Graham was a student at nearby Wheaton College, and one night he called in at the station to tell Shea how much he enjoyed his singing.

Graham later ran a radio programme from the basement of Baptist Church where he was the pastor. Shea sang for the programme, which was called *Songs in the Night*. Shea was also involved in evangelical outreach with Torrey Johnson, founder of Youth for Christ.

George Beverly Shea was a founding director of BGEA, along with Billy Graham, Grady Wilson, George Wilson and choir director Cliff Barrows. He was a regular singer on the BGEA radio programme, *Hour of Decision*, and in all the Billy Graham Crusades. He was still singing up to the age of 104, when he died from complications following a stroke. He was survived by his second wife, Karlene, and two children from his first marriage, Ronnie and Elaine.

Music was always very important in the Billy Graham Crusades. Many famous names from Southern Gospel, Black Gospel and Contemporary Christian Music made regular appearances. But Shea remained the musical mainstay of the crusades. In each crusade, he sang a quiet solo to prepare the people for Graham's message. It was also Shea's idea to have the choir sing softly while the invitation to accept Christ was given at the end. He suggested Graham's well-known sentence "As the choir sings, you come."

The song most commonly sung during the invitation was "Just As I Am," which was written in 1835 by the English poet Charlotte Elliott. Billy Graham wrote that this song presented "the strongest possible Biblical basis for the call of Christ."[73]

Another hymn closely associated with George Beverly Shea and the Billy Graham Crusades was "How Great Thou Art." This was ranked second (after "Amazing Grace") on a list of the favourite hymns of all time in a survey by *Today's Christian* magazine in 2001.

---

[73] The Billy Graham Team, *Crusader Hymns & Hymn Stories*, Minneapolis, MN, 1967, p.33.

"How Great Thou Art"

In 1954, on his first overseas trip, to the Harringay Crusade in London, George Beverly Shea found a song that would be forever linked with him. George Gray, who worked for the Pickering & Inglis publishing firm, gave Shea a copy at a chance encounter in Oxford St. Shea liked it, as did choir director Cliff Barrows, and it was first used in the Toronto Crusade of 1955.

The song was originally written in 1885, in Sweden, by Rev. Carl Boberg, and entitled "O Store Gud" ("O Great God"). It was translated into German and Russian. However, it was an English couple, Mr and Mrs Stuart Hine, who were missionaries to the Ukraine in the 1930s, who translated it into English and added the third and fourth verses.

Amazingly, Dr. J. Edwin Orr heard the hymn being sung by Naga tribespeople in India. He brought the song to the USA, and used it at the Forest Home Christian Conference Center in 1954. Hal Spencer and his sister, Loretta, attended the conference. They took a copy back to their father, Tim Spencer, who published it under the newly-established Manna Music label.

It was in the same year that the copy came into George Beverly Shea's hands. It became a standard at the 1957 New York Crusade. Shea sang it 99 times over the course of the 16-week Crusade. Manna Music also worked with the Billy Graham organisation to make the song freely available to many people.

 "How Great Thou Art"

Stuart Hamblen (1908 - 1989)

One of the most famous converts from the early Billy Graham Crusades was Stuart Hamblen. Hamblen was a very popular radio presenter on the US West

Coast. A singer, songwriter, hunter and cowboy, he had starred with men such as Roy Rogers, Gene Autrey and John Wayne. However, like many famous media personalities, he had serious alcohol and gambling problems. He went to the 1949 Los Angeles Crusade on the invitation of his wife, Suzy. At a private meeting with Billy Graham, he "surrendered his life to Christ." He gave up gambling and drinking and was fired because he would no longer advertise beer. However, he started a new radio programme called *The Cowboy Church of the Air.*

Hamblen's friend John Wayne addressed him at a party, and asked Hamblen point blank, "You've had it tough ever since you got religion, haven't you?" Hamblen answered, "Yes." Wayne followed with, "Do you have any regrets about doing that?" and Hamblen answered with a firm, "NO." Wayne then said, "It's still hard to believe that you would be doing this (practicing Christianity)." To which Hamblen is reported to have replied, "Well, it's no secret what God can do." This stopped Wayne in his tracks and made him think. A bit later, he came back up to Hamblen and said, "You know, that sounds like a good idea for a song."

As well as the song, "It Is No Secret," Hamblen also wrote "They That Wait upon the Lord," "Open up Your Heart and Let the Sunshine In" and "This 'Ole House."

"This 'Ole House" was inspired while Hamblen was on a hunting trip in the High Sierras with a friend. The two men came upon what looked like an abandoned shack, wherein they found the body of an elderly man, apparently dead of natural causes. Hamblen came up with the lyrics to the song while riding horseback down the mountain, and composed the melody within a week. It became his most popular song, but many people did not realise that it was actually expressing the Christian sentiment of growing old, dying and going to be with Jesus in Heaven.

 "It Is No Secret"
"This 'Ole House"
"They That Wait Upon the Lord"

John W. Peterson (1921 – 2006)

During the Second World War, John W. Peterson served as an Army Air Force pilot flying the famed "China Hump."[74] Later, he attended Moody Bible Institute and served on the radio staff there for a number of years. In 1953, he graduated from the American Conservatory of Music in Chicago and shortly thereafter settled in Pennsylvania to continue his song writing career.

He then moved to Grand Rapids, Michigan, where for over ten years he was President and Editor-in-Chief of Singspiration, a sacred music publishing company. He also served on the board of Gospel Films, Inc. of Muskegon, Michigan for several years. Later he moved to Scottsdale, Arizona where he continued his writing and co-founded Good Life Productions. A few years later, the John W. Peterson Music Company was established. During this time, he also served on the board of Family Life Radio Network in Tucson, Arizona.

He had wide experience as a choral director, and throughout his career was in great demand as a guest conductor of his own works. He wrote over 1,000 individual songs, as well as 35 cantatas and musicals.

 "Surely Goodness and Mercy" (with Alfred B. Smith)
"Heaven Came Down"
"Isn't the Love of Jesus Something Wonderful"
"Whisper a Prayer"
"It's Not an Easy Road"
"There's a New Song In My Heart"

---

[74] The "China Hump" involved delivering supplies from India, over the Himalayan Mountains, to support the Chinese war effort.

Gospel Choruses

The 1950s was the great decade of the Gospel Choruses. As the name suggests, these were short songs sung, typically, in Sunday School classes, children's outreach crusades and youth camps.

Singspiration published over 40 song books. This company was started in 1941 by Alfred B. Smith and John W. Peterson. Smith was the first song leader for the Billy Graham Crusades. Singspiration became extremely successful, selling millions of small collections of gospel songs. Zondervan Publishing House purchased Singspiration in 1961 and Brentwood Music purchased Zondervan in the early 1980s.

Here is a small selection of some of the most well-known choruses from this era.

"If You Want Joy"
"For God So Loved the World"
"Rolled Away"
"Ev'rybody Ought to Know"
"Jesus Said that 'Whosoever Will'"

Rock Around the Clock — The 1950s

The 1950s and 60s were completely different decades, yet the cumulative effect was devastating to the Christian church.

The 1950s was generally a family-friendly decade. In the USA, 90 percent of households were made up of families; 86 percent of children lived in a two-parent home and 70 percent of these were biological parents. Almost 60 percent of children were born into a male breadwinner-female homemaker family. Television shows such as *I Love Lucy* served as manuals for successful marriage and child-raising. Church attendances remained high, and the nation was dominated by the middle class, who were square and proud of it![75]

However, there were forces at work that would erupt with devastating effect in the 1960s. One was the Vietnam War. After the defeat of the French and the division of Vietnam into North and South in 1954, the USA was increasingly drawn into the conflict. In the same year, the Supreme Court ruled that segregation in schools was illegal, and ordered all schools to be integrated. Thus began the Civil Rights movement.

Perhaps even more challenging was the rise of a new phenomenon known as the "teenager." Before this, a young person was either a child or an adult, with adult responsibilities. Teenagers now had their own money, which gave them a degree of independence from their parents; they had time – they didn't start work until 17 or 18 – often longer when they did tertiary study; and they were targeted by commercial interests – who were after both their time and their money. "In 1956, there were 13 million teenagers in the USA with a total income of $7 billion a year; the average teenager had a weekly income of $10.55."[76] Unavoidably, "juvenile delinquency" became a major issue of concern. Many feared that the mass media was actually taking control away from parents.

Into this situation came rock 'n' roll. Bill Haley and the Comets' recording of "Rock Around the Clock" topped the charts in 1955. The following year, Elvis Presley exploded on to the scene, selling ten million records. His music and body movements were loud and uninhibited. It was a music that released teenagers from religious and parental restraints and fuelled their mood for rebellion. It was certainly the biggest cultural force in music in the 1950s – arguably in the whole of the twentieth century, and it created a new social revolution.

Ironically, Elvis came from a Pentecostal background. His mother was especially influential in instilling Christianity into him. He would probably have joined a Southern Gospel quartet had he been able to sing harmony. Throughout his life, Gospel music remained his first love. He sang and recorded numerous hymns and Gospel songs, and, until the end, he employed a Southern Gospel

---

[75] Information from Cusic, *op. cit.*, pp. 217 – 219.
[76] *Ibid.*, p. 222.

backing group for his concerts. Forty years after his death, his Gospel songs are still favourites for many older people.

Don Cusic concludes that, "In many ways, Elvis was a phony because he could only sing the message, he could not live it. He remained haunted by gospel music and the gospel itself all his life, but somehow could not reconcile his later life to his boyhood beliefs."[77]

Pat Boone (born 1934)

Pat Boone was second only to Elvis Presley as a chart-topping pop singer in the 1950s and early '60s. He sang mainly cover versions of black rhythm and blues songs and appeared in a number of Hollywood movies. He also wrote a best-selling book for teenagers called *Twixt Twelve and Twenty*. In 1953, when he was only 19 years old, Boone married Shirley Lee Foley, daughter of country music great, Red Foley. The couple had four daughters – Cherry, Lindy, Debby and Laury.

Although brought up as a conservative Christian, Boone almost lost his faith and his marriage in the 1960s. His wife's involvement in the Charismatic Movement, however, eventually influenced Boone to recommit his life to Christ.

The "British Invasion"[78] of the mid-1960s brought an end to Boone's career as a hitmaker. In the 1970s, he switched to Gospel and Country music and founded the record label Lion & Lamb records. He and his family also began attending Jack Hayford's Church on the Way in Van Nuys, California.

Sir Cliff Richard (born Harry Webb 1940)

With his backing group, The Shadows, Cliff Richard dominated the British pop scene in the later 1950s and early 1960s. He became the third top selling artist

---

[77]   *Ibid.*, p.268.
[78]   The "British Invasion" refers to the popularity of British pop music, films and fashions in the USA from the mid-1960s on. Groups such as the Beatles and the Rolling Stones were at the forefront of the invasion.

in the UK Singles Chart history, after the Beatles and Elvis Presley. Although originally cast as a rebellious rock 'n' roll singer, Richard became a professing Christian in 1964. He intended to abandon his singing career, but was persuaded against this. He did, however, soften his music and concentrate more on his Christian faith. He released a number of contemporary Christian albums, and appeared at a number of Billy Graham crusades. In 1967, he starred in the Billy Graham film *Two a Penny*.

Richard has continued to record secular songs, some of which have proved to be controversial. He has also been actively involved in charity work, and regularly gives away at least a tenth of his income. Proceeds from his 1999 single "The Millennium Hymn" went to the charity Children's Promise. This song, which features The Lord's Prayer set to the tune "Auld Lang Syne," reached number one on the UK Singles Chart for three weeks. It also reached number two in Australia and New Zealand.

CHAPTER THIRTEEN

THE ORIGINS OF CONTEMPORARY CHRISTIAN MUSIC

The 1960s — All You Need Is Love

A Hippie

The Hippie counterculture grew out of the post-war "Beat Generation" of writers who advocated experimentation with drugs, alternative forms of sexuality, Eastern religions, communal living and a rejection of materialism. This in turn gave rise to the term "Beatniks" (after Beat Generation and Sputnik[79]). The Beat Generation later became incorporated into the Hippie movement.

The word "Hippie" came from the words 'hip' and 'hep', which were products of African-American culture and denoted someone who was "in the know" or "cool" (as opposed to "square").

The Hippie movement was really a reaction to the materialism and conformity of the preceding decade. According to Billy Graham, it arose as a reaction to "the soulless materialism and the deification of technology in America."[80] It focussed on the positive qualities of love, peace and freedom, but in a generally non-Christian context. It was a search for real meaning in life, amidst the uncertainties of the Cold War and the nuclear threat. The movements it spawned included the anti-Vietnam War movement, the Civil Rights movement, the green movement, and the feminist movement.

Naturally, music played a vital role in the 1960s, as it had in the preceding decade. This was "message" music, and the typical genre was folk rock. In his book, *The Greening of America*, Charles Reich described the new music as "The chief medium of expression, the chief means by which inner feelings are communicated."[81] Song titles such as "He's Not Heavy, He's My Brother"; "Bridge Over Troubled Waters"; "All You Need is Love"; "Give Peace a Chance"; "Where Have all the Flowers Gone?" "If I Had a Hammer" and "I'd Like to Teach the World to Sing" expressed the sentiments of the era.

Some songs that rated highly on the charts were actually revivals of old Gospel songs, while others had "Christian" words in them, although they were not necessarily sung by Christians. Examples of songs with a Christian theme

---

[79] The first space satellite, launched by the Soviet Union in 1957.
[80] Billy Graham, *The Jesus Generation*, Zondervan, Grand Rapids, Michigan,1971, p. 20.
[81] Charles Reich, *The Greening of America*, Allen Lane The Penguin Press, London, 1971, p.178.

included "Michael Row Your Boat Ashore"; "Turn, Turn, Turn"[82]; "I Believe"; "People Get Ready"; "Put Your Hand in the Hand"; "Day by Day"; "Morning Has Broken" and "Jesus Is Just Alright."

Musicals, such as *Joseph and the Amazing Technicolour Dreamcoat, Jesus Christ Superstar* and *Godspell* were part of the general ferment of spiritual ideas in this era, although, theologically, they were somewhat unorthodox.

The Jesus Movement was born out of the Hippie Movement (the term Jesus Freaks was originally used by non-Christian Hippies to describe those who had converted to Christianity). The Movement started in 1967, when Ted Wise and John MacDonald opened a coffee shop called The Living Room in the Haight-Ashbury district of San Francisco.[83] The young baby-boomers "readily embraced the warm, loving God of the '60s who was concerned about peace, love, social justice, and most importantly, each individual's life."[84]

The Jesus Movement spawned a whole culture of coffee houses, rock festivals, poster art, radio shows and magazines. Countless young people sat around campfires at Bible camps and youth meetings, singing songs such as "Kumbaya," "Amen," "Give Me Oil in My Lamp," "When the Saints Go Marching In," "Do Lord," "Go Tell It on the Mountain," and other sing-along type songs, which never made it inside the doors of established churches.

Artists and groups such as the Spurrlows, the Continentals[85], Love Song, Larry Norman, Randy Stonehill, Mylon LeFevre, Randy Matthews, Agape and the All Saved Freak Band became the forerunners of the Contemporary Christian Music scene. When they were criticised by more conservative churchgoers,

---

[82] The Byrds' recording of Pete Seeger's paraphrase of Ecclesiastes 3, "Turn, Turn Turn," reached #1 on the hit parades on October 23, 1965.

[83] Shimon Galiley, "Jesus Music: The Story of the Jesus Movement and Evaluation of Its Musical Impact," Senior Honors Thesis, Liberty University, 2011, pp. 13-14. Haight-Ashbury was one of the main centres of Hippie culture. It grew very popular after the release of Scott McKenzie's rendition of the song "San Francisco (Be Sure To Wear Flowers in Your Hair)" in 1967.

[84] Cusic, *op.cit.*, p. 243.

[85] Both the Spurrlows (founded by Thurlow Spurr) and the Continentals (founded by Cam Floria) grew out of the Youth for Christ movement in the early 1960s.

they responded with the question – "Why should the devil have all the good music?"[86]

Calvary Chapel, pastored by Chuck Smith and Lonnie Frisbee (a converted Hippie), was one of the few churches that embraced the Jesus Movement. Thousands of young people, including many musicians, attended the Chapel. Maranatha! Music was formed as a channel for their talent. It became a leader in "praise and worship" music, but its first album was a live recording of *The Everlastin' Living Jesus Concert*. The members of the rock group Love Song were saved and delivered from the drug scene at Calvary Chapel in 1969, and they became the Chapel's official band, and went on to release the first "hit" album of the Jesus Movement, called *Love Song*.

The Artists

Larry Norman

Larry Norman (1947 - 2008)

Larry Norman was always a controversial figure. Dubbed the "original Jesus rocker," and
the "father of Christian rock music," he was
known for his signature long hair and the "One
Way Jesus" finger pointed heavenward. Released by Capitol Records in 1969, *Upon This Rock* became the first commercially released Jesus rock album.

Watch or listen to Larry Norman singing one of the following
"I Wish We'd All Been Ready"
"The Rock that Doesn't Roll"

---

[86] Apparently there is no proof that Martin Luther, John Wesley or William Booth made this statement. The closest we can get is a remark made by Rev. Rowland Hill, when he arranged an Easter hymn to the tune of "Pretty, Pretty Polly Hopkins", in *The Rambler*, Vol. 9, 1858, p. 191. Hill is reported to have said, "The Devil should not have all the best tunes."

"Sweet, Sweet Song of Salvation"
"Why Should the Devil have all the Good Music?"

Mylon Lefevre (born 1944)

Mylon LeFevre performed Gospel with his family from a young age and was a member of the LeFevre Singers. One of his early songs, "Without Him," was recorded by Elvis Presley. The stresses of his rock 'n' roll lifestyle led him into drugs, but he recommitted his life to Christ in the late 1970s.

Randy Matthews (born 1952)

Randy Matthews was born into a family with at least five ordained ministers, including his father, Monty, who was a founding member of the Jordanaires.[87] After attending Bible College, he began ministering to street people from a coffee shop called "The Jesus House" in Cincinnati. In 1971, he was signed as the first contemporary Christian artist to record for Word Records. His first album, *Wish We'd All Been Ready*, was quite radical for its time. Word then launched a new label, Myrrh Records to cater for the new Jesus rock music. Randy Matthews' *All I Am Is What You See* was one of its premier albums.

Phil Keaggy (born 1951)

Phil Keaggy was born into a family of ten children on a small farm in Hubbard, Ohio. An accident at the age of four cost him half of the middle finger on his right hand.

Initially attracted to the drums, he was given a guitar instead, and during the 1960s he played in a number of bands, including Glass Harp. Although he left the band in 1972, they have played together on a number of occasions since then.

---

[87] The Jordanaires were a gospel group. They sang together from 1948 to 2013. Between 1956 and 1970 they provided background vocals for Elvis Presley.

By the end of the 1960s, Keaggy was heavily into drugs and having nightmares. After his mother, who was a devout Catholic Christian, was killed in a car accident in 1970, he followed the advice of his older sister, Ellen, and committed his life to Christ.

After recording three successful albums with Glass Harp, which included some material that he had written as a new Christian, Keaggy left the band to pursue a solo career.

In 1973, he married Bernadette, and the couple had three children, Alicia, Olivia and Ian, after losing five babies (including a set of triplets) either before or shortly after birth. Bernadette tells this story in her book *A Deeper Shade of Grace*, updated in 1996 to *Losing You Too Soon*.

Phil and Bernadette moved to Upstate New York to become part of Love Inn Community, led by disk-jockey Scott Ross. Sadly, the community became affiliated with the authoritarian Shepherding Movement.

After extricating himself from Love Inn, Keaggy's second solo album, *Love Broke Thru*', included the first recording of the song "Your Love Broke Through," written by Keith Green, Todd Fishkind and Randy Stonehill. It also included the extended song "Time," which contained some innovative guitar work.

One of his most acclaimed albums is the instrumental *The Master and the Musician*, released in 1978. A second instrumental album *The Wind and the Wheat*, earned Keaggy his first Dove Award in 1988. His second Dove Award came in 1992 for his Celtic-influenced, *Beyond Nature*. Altogether, he has released over 50 solo albums and won seven Dove Awards.

In 1995, 1996, and 1997 Keaggy was voted the number two Best Acoustic Fingerstyle Guitarist in the *Guitar Player Magazine* readers' poll. The title track of one of his best-selling albums, *True Believer*, reached number one on the Christian radio charts in 1995. He has also been voted the Greatest Christian Rock Guitarist of All Time by Classic Christian Rock Zone.[88]

In 1984, Keaggy and Randy Stonehill co-wrote and sang the duet "Who Will Save the Children?" for Stonehill's album *Celebrate This Heartbeat*. The duet would also serve as a theme song for Compassion International, which both artists support.

---

[88]   <www.classicchristianrockzine.com> Accessed July 13, 2017.

Talking about his 2002 album *Hymnsongs,* Keaggy said ""I've always loved hymns. They're great melodies that still stand on their own, and are still sung, even after centuries have passed. And those melodies are even more appreciated when you know the lyrics. The writers of the hymns were great wordsmiths; they could be so concise and so eloquent in their expression of truth. And theirs is music that speaks to every generation."[89]

Jesus Festivals

The culmination of the Jesus Movement was Explo '72 – "The Christian Woodstock." This event was the brainchild of Campus Crusade for Christ founder, Bill Bright. His aim was to train 100,000 young people in evangelism, and send them out to train five other people. An army of lay evangelists would then evangelise America by 1976, and the world by 1980[90].

The event was held in Dallas, Texas, and 80,000 "delegates" came for the four days of workshops. The main speaker was Billy Graham. On the last day, an estimated 180,000 attended an all-day concert featuring artists such as Johnny Cash, Kris Kristofferson, Randy Matthews, Barry McGuire, Reba Rambo, Larry Norman, Love Song and Andrae Crouch and the Disciples.

There are a number of videos on YouTube featuring excerpts from Explo '72. There are also longer documentaries on the whole Jesus Movement, e.g. The Jesus People film (1972) <https://www.youtube.com/watch?v=XmUvnN3mtuc>

Explo '72 was not the first major Jesus festival. Six thousand people had gathered for the Faith Festival in Evansville, Indiana, in March 1970. Pat Boone and his family were the leading performers. The event was repeated in 1971. Later in 1970, the Love Song Festival at Knotts Berry Farm drew 20,000 people. The success of this event prompted the proprietors to stage more Christian

---

[89] Mark Moring, "The Musician Is a Master," *Christianity Today,* May 6, 2013.
[90] Larry Eskridge, *God's Forever Family: The Jesus People Movement in America, 1966-1977,* Stirling, Scotland, University of Stirling, 2005, p. 235.

music nights. These were eventually renamed Maranatha Night at Knotts, due to the use of music groups from Calvary Chapel.[91]

In August 1973, a Mennonite, Harold Zimmerman, organised Jesus '73 in a central Pennsylvania potato field. Eight thousand people attended what was to become an annual event. "The music they heard, in many cases for the first time, was contemporary Christian music. As each person returned home, the news of Jesus music spread."[92] The organisers, however, had wanted a family friendly festival, and they found the music "too racy." The following year the audience had doubled in size, but the famous event occurred in which Randy Matthews was unplugged in the middle of his set and, apparently, driven off the stage by some enraged festival-goers.

1975 was the year when Jesus festivals sprang up throughout the country. Cam Floria and Bill Rayborn organised the First Annual Christian Artists' Seminar in the Rockies, for those involved in music ministry. This eventually became known simply as "Estes Park." Other festivals held that year included Salt '75 in Michigan, Fishnet '75 at Front Royal, Virginia, the Sonshine Festival in Ohio, the Road Home Celebration in Colorado Springs, and the Hill Country Faith Festival in Texas.

There were also Jesus Festivals in other parts of the world, some of which are still running today. In the United Kingdom, the Greenbelt Festival, which began in 1974, was one of the world's largest Christian events. It has lost some of its Christian flavour today. Festivals continue in a number of European countries. The Halleluya Festival is a large Catholic festival in Brazil, while the Parachute Music Festival, which ran in New Zealand from 1992 to 2014, was the largest Christian festival in the Southern Hemisphere.

All of these festivals attracted some criticism from church members, but much of the criticism was blunted when young people returned home filled with joy and a new zeal for soul winning.

---

[91]   Peter Baker, *Contemporary Christian Music: Where It Came from, What It Is, and Where It's Going*, Crossway Books, Westchester, Illinois, 1985, p. 84.

[92]   *Ibid.*, p. 85.

The Media

These were also the years when Christian radio stations began, very tentatively, to play contemporary Christian music. One of the very first shows was *The Scott Ross Show*, which began broadcasting in 1969. Ross was a long-haired disc jockey, who had recently become a Christian. He had a burden to reach young people with the love of Jesus, and he was able to partner with Pat Robertson, the head of the Christian Broadcasting Network (CBN). Within a few years, *The Scott Ross Show* was being broadcast on 175 stations nationwide.

Another nationally syndicated Jesus music show was Paul Baker's *A Joyful Noise*, which ran for eleven years, from 1970 to 1981. Other dee-jays played as much Jesus music as they could get away with, which was often not very much! It was not until 1975 that the first all-Jesus-music radio stations began in Santa Ana, California (KYMS, the "Spirit of 106"), Lincoln, Nebraska (KBHL, "The Sound of New Life"), and Houston, Texas (KFMK).

The 1960s and 70s also produced a number of contemporary Christian films and musicals. In an attempt to address the issues of the day, Billy Graham's organisation World Wide Pictures produced a film called *The Restless Ones* in 1965. The film's theme was the "rebellious teenager," and it is estimated that two million people watched it in the first year, resulting in over 120,000 conversions.[93]

Ralph Carmichael wrote the music for *The Restless Ones*, as well as for a number of other Billy Graham films. One of the most famous songs from *The Restless Ones* is "He's Everything to Me." This is sung around a beach campfire. The lyrics tell how we can know *about* God, but not know Him personally until we accept His grace extended to us through Jesus Christ.

Watch a video clip of the scene from *The Restless Ones* featuring the song "He's Everything to Me."

---

[93] Peter T. Chattaway, "Billy Graham Goes to the Movies" *Patheos*, August 23, 2005, <http://www.patheos.com/blogs/filmchat/2005/08/billy-graham-goes-to-the-movies.html>

Ralph Carmichael (born 1927) and Kurt Kaiser (born 1934)

Ralph Carmichael is the son of a Pentecostal minister. As a result of listening to the radio at a young age, he became convinced that there was more to Christian music than he was hearing in most churches. His father, who played the trombone and ragtime piano, encouraged him to learn the violin, piano and trumpet.

"How can you sing about the joy of the Lord," Carmichael pondered, "when you can only use the organ or the piano? You couldn't sing about the joy of the Lord using instruments like in the Old Testament – the drums, the cymbals, the sackbut, the stringed instrument, or the loud sounding brass! It didn't make sense to me! Did God change His mind somewhere between the Old Testament and the New Testament?"[94]

After leaving school he studied for the ministry at Southern California Bible College (Vanguard University). While at college, he spent much of his time organising and writing arrangements for bands. He was particularly attracted to the Big Band style of the 1940s.

His contemporary arrangements of hymns and Gospel songs, as well as secular songs, attracted much criticism from conservative Christians, but brought him to the attention of recording executives at Capitol records. As a result, he worked with many famous singers of the time, including Pat Boone, Rosemary Clooney, Nat King Cole, Bing Crosby and Ella Fitzgerald. He also wrote musical scores for TV shows such as *I Love Lucy*, *Bonanza* and *Roy Rogers and Dale Evans*.

Carmichael wrote the music for about twenty Billy Graham films, including *For Pete's Sake*, *World's Fair Encounter*, *His Land*, *The Heart is a Rebel* and *The Cross and the Switchblade*.

Watch video clips of a young Cliff Richard singing Ralph Carmichael's songs "His Land" and "The New 23rd" from the movie *His Land*. You can also watch "Hallelujah" (an arrangement of the "Hallelujah Chorus") from the same movie.

---

[94] Quoted in Paul Baker, *op. cit.*, p. 13.

As the Jesus Movement took hold in the 1960s, Carmichael wanted to write something his teenage daughter, Carol, could relate to. The result was a number of church musicals, written in collaboration with the talented piano player and record producer **Kurt Kaiser.**

The first musical, *Tell It Like It Is* (1969) included the famous song "Pass It On." *Natural High* and *I'm Here, God's Here, Now We Can Start* followed. These musicals were built around modern folk and folk/rock instrumentation, and they introduced what became known as Contemporary Christian Music into the church. "It was the beginning of youth finding a place in church again," said Carmichael.

"Love Is Surrender" is another song from *Tell It Like It Is*. This song was an answer to those who advocated love as the answer to all of society's ills. The message of the song is that you can talk and sing about love all you like. You can even shout that wars will end because all men are brothers. However, outside of Jesus Christ, you cannot find true love. Real, lasting love is only to be found when you surrender your life to the will of God.

 "Pass It On"
"Love Is Surrender"

It was his desire to provide a wider market for the music of the Jesus People, and a vehicle for the new musical genre he had helped to create, which led Carmichael to found Light Records/Lexicon Music in 1966. Light was responsible for launching the careers of some of the pioneers of CCM, including Andrae Crouch, the Winans, Dino, Reba Rambo, Jamie Owens and Carman.

 Watch a video clip of Ralph Carmichael leading a Big Band

 Sing or listen to the popular songs by Ralph Carmichael and Kurt Kaiser "Oh How He Loves You and Me"

"Reach Out to Jesus"
"Something Good Is Going to Happen to You" (Oral Robert's theme song)
"I Looked for Love"

SCRIPTURE IN SONG

Although Maranatha! Music is well known for its praise and worship music, one of the most powerful and long-lasting contributions came from the small country of New Zealand.

In 1968, Dave and Dale Garratt produced a small EP (extended play) album containing nine new songs. The album was called *Scripture in Song*. The Garratts were not musicians, but they were worshippers, longing to lead the people of God into a new encounter with the Holy Spirit.

This was the time of the Charismatic Renewal. Many people within the mainline churches were coming into the experience of the Baptism of the Holy Spirit, which had long been the sole preserve of the Pentecostals. Simple new worship songs, often based on Scripture, were being written by ordinary men and women under the influence of the Holy Spirit. It was these songs that the Garratts sought to incorporate into their new style of Christian music.

Over the next 25 years, they produced 30 albums and a number of song books. Some of the songs were written by the Garratts themselves, while others were drawn from song writers in New Zealand and around the world. Many of the songs were completely anonymous.

The songs were tuneful and easily memorised. The early albums featured simple accompaniments of piano, guitar and drums. Attempts to incorporate these instruments into mainline church services often met with strong opposition, however. In the end, many of these churches adopted a compromise solution of having two services, one traditional and the other more contemporary. This is a practice that still continues to the present day.

Sing or listen to a selection of Scripture in Song. Here are a few suggestions.

"From the Rising of the Sun"

"My Glory and the Lifter of My Head"

"Therefore the Redeemed of the Lord"

"Seek Ye First the Kingdom of God"

"I Exalt Thee" (by Pete Sanchez)

"Be Exalted O God" (This famous song was written by New Zealander Brent Chambers. Chambers also wrote "Song of Offering," "Celebration Song" and "Chosen People.")

"Majesty" (This famous song was written by Jack Hayford, senior pastor of Church on the Way, Van Nuys, California. Hayford wrote a number of other songs, including "Praise Him, Praise Him, God of Creation." Pat Boone and his family, Jimmy Owens and his family, and the Wards – Matthew and Nelly, with their sister Annie and her husband Buck Herring – all worshiped at the Church on the Way at various times.

CHAPTER FOURTEEN

CONTEMPORARY CHRISTIAN MUSIC IN THE 70S AND 80S

The Fourth Great Awakening

In his famous essay published as the cover story in the August 23, 1976 issue of *New York* magazine, Tom Wolfe described the 1970s as the "'Me' Decade." He saw a shift from a communitarian type of society to a more individualized one, where the emphasis was on self and self-help. This would continue into the 1980s, which would become known as the "My Decade" because of the emphasis on the possession of material goods.

Although the concept is not universally accepted, some writers[95] have seen the 1960s and 70s as a Fourth Great Awakening. There was a decline in traditional mainstream church membership, while other groups, such as Southern Baptists, Missouri Synod Lutherans, Pentecostals, Holiness groups and Nazarenes, grew rapidly. The Jesus Movement and the Charismatic Renewal are generally included in this Awakening, as is the ministry of world leaders such as Billy Graham, Pope John Paul II and Martin Luther King Jnr.

---

[95] Most notably economic historian Robert Fogel, in his 2000 book *The Fourth Great Awakening and the Future of Egalitarianism.*

As Don Cusic has said, "America underwent a spiritual awakening, and Christianity that was fundamental in its beliefs, active in its faith, and in touch with the contemporary culture became acceptable."[96]

Christians in the late 1970s spoke of the decade as the "'We' Decade." Following on from the 1976 election of Jimmy Carter, a "born again" evangelical Christian, as President of the USA, they embarked on a period of social activism, targeting especially the "gay" rights movement, abortion, and the attack on the teaching of creationism in schools.

In South Australia, the Festival of Light was formed in 1973 to "make a stand against moral decline." The following year, Uniting Church minister, Fred Nile, was appointed full-time New South Wales director. In 1981, representing the Call to Australia Party, he was elected to the Legislative Council of the New South Wales Parliament.

In New Zealand, the Society for the Protection of the Unborn Child (SPUC) was formed in 1970, under the leadership of foetal surgeon, Professor William Liley. In 1972, a series of "Jesus Marches' took place throughout New Zealand, as Christians stood up for Biblical standards of righteousness and virtue.

The 1970s was also the decade when Christianity became a marketable commodity. Christian book shops spread throughout the land, selling a wide range of Christian products. In America, the Gospel Music Association, at the suggestion of Bill Gaither, had established the Dove Awards for Gospel music. The first awards ceremony had been held in 1969. For the first few years, most of the awards went to Southern Gospel singers.

The Artists

Jimmy and Carol Owens are a married couple who pioneered Contemporary Christian Music during the 1970s and 80s. Married since 1954, they have two adult children in ministry. Jamie Owens-Collins is a well-known recording artist, songwriter and speaker and Buddy Owens is an author and a Teaching Pastor at Saddleback Church in Lake Forest, California.

---

96   Cusic, *op.cit.*, p. 281.

The Owens have been responsible for a number of very popular Christian musicals, such as *Come Together – A Musical Experience in Love* (1972), *If My People: A Musical Experience in Worship and Intercession* (1974), *The Witness* (1978), *The Victor* (1984) and *Heal Our Land: Praise and Prayer to Change a Nation* (1995). The original recordings of *Come Together* and *If My People* featured Pat Boone, 2nd Chapter of Acts, Jamie Owens and Barry McGuire. McGuire also played Peter in *The Witness*.

Jimmy and Carol Owens

The *Victor* tells the story of Christ's resurrection and his Second Coming. It features additional songs by Jamie Owens-Collins ("The Battle Belongs to the Lord"), Annie Herring ("Easter Song") and Don Francisco ("He's Alive").

The classic musical for children, *Ants'hillvania* (1981), written with Cherry Boone O'Neill (oldest daughter of Pat and Shirley Boone), was both a Grammy and a Dove Award Finalist as best recording for children.

 "Freely, Freely" (from *Come Together*)
"Holy, Holy" (from *Come Together*)
"Life Giver/You Are the Christ" (from *The Witness*)
"If My People"
"The Victor"
"The Battle Belongs to the Lord" (from *The Victor*)
"He's Alive" (from *The Victor*)

Barry McGuire (born 1935)

Barry McGuire was born in the USA. After various jobs as a fisherman and pipe fitter, he started singing for a living. He and Barry Kane formed a duo singing folk music. They also toured with the New Christy Minstrels.

In 1963, he and the Minstrels' founder, Randy Sparks, co-wrote what would be the group's greatest hit – "Green, Green It's Green They Say."

As a solo folk rock singer during the 1960s, he scored a hit with his song "Eve of Destruction." However, like many other singers of this era, he was deeply involved in the drug culture.

He gave his life to Christ in 1971, after hearing evangelist Arthur Blessitt[97] speaking. Since then he has written a number of well-known Christian songs, including "Bullfrogs and Butterflies," "Soldiers of the Army" and "Communion Song."

McGuire married a New Zealander called Mari, who was a former secretary of Winki Pratney.

Listen to Barry McGuire singing
"Bullfrogs and Butterflies"
"Communion Song"

2nd Chapter of Acts

2nd Chapter of Acts (Matthew Ward, Nelly Greisen and Annie Herring)

---

[97] Arthur Blessitt was called the "Minister of Sunset Strip" in Hollywood. He preached to hippies and drug addicts, and opened a coffee shop called His Place. He is best known for carrying a 12-foot cross through every country on Earth. This is the subject of a recently released DVD called simply *The Cross*.

Annie Ward (born 1945) lost both her parents in the later 1960s, and she and her husband, record engineer Buck Herring, took in her younger siblings, Nelly and Matthew. The three Wards began to sing together, eventually coming to the attention of Pat Boone, who arranged a recording contract for two singles. They also provided backing vocals for Barry McGuire's first two Christian albums, which were produced by Buck Herring.

Naming themselves the 2nd Chapter of Acts (the chapter in the Bible that tells the story of the outpouring of the Holy Spirit on the day of Pentecost), they released their debut album in 1974. The album contained Annie Herring's "Easter Song." The group recorded several albums for Myrrh Records, before moving, in 1978, to the new Sparrow label, which had been started by Billy Ray Hearn.

2nd chapter of Acts recorded many songs that became part of the burgeoning Jesus music genre that formed the foundation of Contemporary Christian Music.

When the 2nd Chapter of Acts disbanded in 1988, Annie and Matthew continued with solo careers. Nelly, who had married film producer/distributor Steve Greisen in 1978, devoted her life to helping her husband and bringing up their two sons. Matthew and his wife, Deanne, have three daughters: Megin, Morgan, and Mattie.

You can listen to Annie Herring giving her testimony at https://www.youtube.com/watch?v=bwY24lY1pN4.

If possible, listen to a live performance by 2nd Chapter of Acts singing
"Easter Song"
"Mansion Builder"

Petra

Petra was a Christian rock band that was formed in 1972 by Bob Hartman, at the Christian Training Academy, in Fort Wayne, Indiana. Billy Ray Hearn signed the group to his new Myrrh label and released its first album in 1974. Because the music was loud and powerful, it was not well received by most Christian radio stations and bookstores. Three more albums released by Myrrh and Star Song between 1977 and 1981 also had limited success, although they did produce the hit songs "Why Should the Father Bother" and "The Coloring Song." Both songs were quite mellow by rock standards, but they did introduce Petra to a wider audience, and "The Coloring Song" reached number one on three Christian radio charts.

The group's breakthrough came in 1981, when they were asked to tour with the group Servant. Other national tours followed. The tours boosted sales for the fourth album, sometime after its first release. They also provided a platform for the release of the fifth album, *More Power to Ya*. This album was noteworthy for its deliberate use of backmasking (a recording technique in which a sound or message is recorded backward on to a track that is meant to be played forward). This technique had been used by secular artists such as the Beatles, Led Zeppelin and Pink Floyd, and some conservative church leaders believed that it was being used by Christian artists to hide subliminal Satanic messages. Petra inserted a blatant message, backmasked between two tracks. The message said, "What are you looking for the devil for when you oughta be looking for the Lord?"

Over 33 years, Petra recorded more than 20 albums and won four Grammy and ten Dove Awards. As their focus shifted from winning converts to encouraging and exhorting believers, the theme of spiritual warfare became more explicit in their songs, with albums such as *This Means War! On Fire!* and *Wake-Up Call*.

After many changes of personnel, the band finally disbanded in 2006, although they have continued to perform and record on occasions, sometimes under the name of Classic Petra.

In 2004, *CCM Magazine* noted that "Few artists had as much influence in the formation and growth of what has come to be known as 'contemporary Christian music' as did Petra. . . . As one of the movement's trailblazers, Petra bore the brunt of the controversy, enduring picketers, protesters and public denunciations by prominent Christian leaders. . . . Still, all rabble-rousers aside, Petra managed to create some of Christian music's most treasured recordings."[98]

Petra members before disbanding in 2006 (l–r): Greg
Bailey, Bob Hartman, John Schlitt, Paul Simmons

Watch or listen to Petra live. You may choose one of the following, or a more rock style:
"The Coloring Song"
"We Want To See Jesus Lifted High"
"Why Should the Father Bother"

---

[98] "CCM Hall of Fame: Petra," *CCM Magazine*, 2004.

Scott Wesley Brown (born 1952)

In a career spanning over four decades, Scott Wesley Brown has been singer, songwriter, worship leader, mission enthusiast and church planter.

He has recorded 25 albums (mostly for Sparrow Records) and has visited over 50 countries. He has been active in mission work, supplying musical instruments to people in Third World countries. He is currently senior pastor of Sonship Community Church in Southern California.

Brown is married to Belinda and has two daughters.

 "I Wish You Jesus"
"Learning to Live Like Jesus"
"He Will Carry You"

Keith Green

Keith Green (1953 – 1982)

One early CCM artist who exemplifies the whole 1960s culture is Keith Green. Green had a Jewish background, but he was brought up in Christian Science. At 11 years old, he and his father signed a five-year recording contract with Decca Records. The first song released on disc was Green's own composition, "A Go-Go Getter." The recording company aimed at making Green a teenager rock star, but the dream never materialised.

As a young person in the late 1960s and 1970s Green tried drugs, Eastern religions and "free love." "I'm like a person at a train station watching all the trains of thought go by and I'm not getting on any of them," he said. When he gave up drugs after a bad trip and started reading about Jesus, the Gospel penetrated his heart.

Although he had accepted Christianity, he had not yet been born again. So when he met his future wife, Melody, who was also Jewish, and moved in with her, the relationship was extremely volatile. Nevertheless, Keith and Melody got married in 1973 and began attending a Bible study at Vineyard Church[99]. Keith committed his life to Christ in 1975 and Melody followed soon after.

As with everything else, Green gave total commitment to his new faith. His songs changed from searching to "Here it is – I've found the answer."

 "You Put This Love in My Heart"
"Your Love Broke Through"

Eager to put Christ's teaching into practice, the Greens started bringing people who needed help into their home in Los Angeles. Eventually they owned two houses and rented another five to accommodate all the people they were helping and counselling. (At one stage there were 65 people.) Eventually they bought their own property in Texas, where they founded Last Days Ministries.

As a Christian, Green could not get signed with any major secular record companies, so he agreed to sign with Sparrow Records and concentrate on Christian music. He'd always wanted to be a pop star. Now he only wanted to communicate God's Word.

He soon found himself at the forefront of popular Christian music, and that presented him with a dilemma. His one aim was to point people to the Lord; he didn't want to be applauded himself. He saw his concerts as very much a ministry, and he would spend quite a lot of time preaching and exhorting the audience to turn to Christ. Many of his songs had very pointed and confrontational lyrics.

 "To Obey is Better than Sacrifice"

He soon realised that he was offending people for the wrong reason and asked God to help him control his "radical tendencies."

---

99 Under the leadership of John Wimber, Vineyard Church founded the record label Vineyard Music in 1985.

He could not accept the idea that people should pay to hear the Gospel in his concerts. This was a very controversial move. Most other Christian artists were happy with the concept of living off the Gospel. After re-signing with Sparrow, he felt that he had compromised by selling the Gospel for a profit, so he went to Billy Ray Hearn and asked to be let out of his contract. From then on he produced and sold his records for whatever people could pay – if they couldn't pay then they were free.

After a trip overseas visiting ministry bases, he and Melody got a vision for overseas missions, however this vision was never to be fulfilled in his own life. On July 28, 1982, Green, his two sons and the entire Smalley family (mother, father and six children) were killed in a small plane crash. Green was 28 years old.

 "Jesus Commands Us to Go"

Green's second album was called *No Compromise* and that was the theme of his life. It was also the name that his wife gave to the biography she wrote of him after his death. As he said in the book *A Cry in the Wilderness*, "It doesn't make any sense to be a Christian and not be Christian – to call Him Lord but not do what He says."[100]

Green's songs have been re-recorded many times since his death. Most importantly, however, countless thousands of people have committed their lives to global missions as a result of his ministry.

 "Create in Me a Clean Heart"
"Oh Lord, You're Beautiful"
"There is a Redeemer" (Melody Green wrote this song)

---

[100] Keith Green, *A Cry in the Wilderness*, Word Publishing, Milton Keynes, 1993, p. 146.

You can watch an hour long video of Keith Green's life. See *Your Love Broke Through*, or *The Keith Green Story*.

"I repent of ever having recorded one single song, and ever having performed one concert, if my music, and more importantly, my life has not provoked you into Godly jealousy (Romans 11:11) or to sell out more completely to Jesus! . . . the only music minister to whom the Lord will say, 'Well done, thou good and faithful servant," is the one whose life proves what their lyrics are saying, and to whom music is the least important part of their life. Glorifying the only worthy One has to be a minister's most important goal!"

Keith Green, "So You Wanna Be a Rock Star," Last Days Ministries, <http://www.lastdaysministries.org/Groups/1000008644/Last_Days_Ministries/Keith_Green/Keith_Green.aspx>

B. J. Thomas (born 1942)

By 1975, B. J. Thomas had recorded a string of hits, including "Raindrops Keep Fallin' on My Head," from the movie *Butch Cassidy and the Sundance Kid*. Privately, however, his life was spiralling out of control due to drug addiction. After a near-death experience, Thomas, with the support of his wife and daughter, accepted

B.J. Thomas, 1972

Christ as his Saviour. He was miraculously delivered from his addiction and began to sing Christian songs for the Myrrh label.

Other famous pop stars who affirmed their faith in Christ during these years included Johnny Cash, Noel Paul Stookey (of Peter, Paul and Mary fame) and Glen Campbell. Bob Dylan converted to Christianity in the late 1970s, but he later distanced himself from any organised religion.

Evie Tornquist (born 1956)

Evie

The 1977 and 1978 Dove Awards for Best Female Vocalist went to Evie Tornquist. Evie, as she was known, was, in many ways, the first CCM "star." Born to Norwegian immigrant parents, she started singing as a young teenager. Altogether, she recorded 30 albums, several of which sold over 100,000 copies. Her sweet voice endeared her to many people, and it was thought that she would be the one to take Contemporary Christian Music to the secular market. However, in 1979, she married Swedish pastor Pelle Karlsson. Two years later, she retired from performing and recording to raise two children and pursue other areas of ministry.

In the mid 2000s, however, she toured the USA with Australian singer, Rebecca St. James, doing a series of concerts and events for women entitled SHE: Safe, Healthy and Empowered.

Listen to Evie singing songs such as "Give Them All to Jesus" and "Step into the Sunshine."

Debby Boone (born 1956) has a similar story. She is the third of four daughters born to Pat and Shirley Boone. After singing Gospel with other members of her family, Boone recorded her first solo song "You Light up My Life" (1977). The song became an instant hit and was the top selling recording of the 1970s. Despite being billed as a love song, Boone has stated that she sang it to God.

Later songs failed to reach this level of popularity, and Boone concentrated more on Country Music and Contemporary Christian Music. She also toured the country in a number of popular stage musicals.

In 1979, she married Gabriel Ferrer, and the couple had four children. In 2005, after raising her family, she returned to the recording studio, producing a CD that paid tribute to her mother-in-law, 1950s pop star Rosemary Clooney.

 Listen to Debby Boone singing "You Light up My Life."

The Eighties

By the 1980s, some of the glitter was beginning to wear off the Contemporary Christian Music scene. Part of the problem was inadequate spiritual covering. This meant that Christian artists often lacked accountability to a pastor, friend or mentor. One of the results of this was burn-out, and this sometimes led on to more serious marital difficulties or drug and alcohol addictions, which affected all genres of Christian music.[101] Because of the preoccupation with self in the 1970s (the "me" decade), these moral problems were often covered up or glossed over.

Don Francisco (born 1946) who wrote the song "He's Alive," was one who admitted to suffering from burnout in the mid-1980s. "I was getting to the point," he admitted "where I was saying things on the stage that I knew I believed, but I knew they weren't a part of my life anymore."[102] He further warned that God would destroy any ministry that did not bring people into a heart relationship with Jesus.

Dallas Holm (born 1948) issued a call to holiness, as an antidote to burnout. "As I look at a lot of contemporary Christianity, I don't see too much that I would define as holiness. On the contrary, I see a very disturbing trend of people seeking to be accepted by the world, applying the world's methods and standards to Christianity, rather than the other way around. I see a lot of letting down of

---

[101] See, for example, Donnie Sumner on page 150.
[102] Quoted in Baker, *op.cit.*, p. 166.

the standards, a lot of permissiveness, and a lot of watering down of the Gospel ... As I read the words of Scripture, and as I take them and apply them literally to my own life, I realize that I have to undergo a revolutionary, radical change in my whole way of thinking."[103]

 Listen to Dallas Holm singing "Rise Again."

Sandi Patty (born 1956)

Sandi Patty started singing at the age of two, but she was 23 before she recorded her first professional album for Singspiration! Her career skyrocketed, especially after she won two Dove Awards – for Artist of the Year and Female Vocalist of the Year – in 1982. She subsequently sang backup for the Bill Gaither Trio and launched her own national tours as a solo performer. Dubbed "The Voice," by the late 1980s she was performing over 200 concerts a year and employing a staff of 30 to manage her career.

By her own admission, however, she was using her ministry career as a substitute for a spiritual relationship with God. Later she stated, "You think that's a replacement for a relationship, and it is not; that is a lesson I have learned the hard way."[104]

In truth, Patty was leading a private life far removed from her public profile. A very public divorce and remarriage in the mid-1990s led to a confession of adultery. In interviews and in her biography *Broken on the Back Row*, Patty genuinely sought to make amends for the harm she had done.

---

[103] *Ibid.* Holm won four Dove awards in 1977 - Song of the Year: "Rise Again," Songwriter of the Year, Male Vocalist of the Year and Mixed Group of the Year (Dallas Holm and Praise)

[104] Timothy C. Morgan, "Sandi Patty Stages Comeback," *Christianity Today*, January 12, 1998, <http://www.christianitytoday.com/ct/1998/january12/8t156a.html?ctlredirect=true>.

Although her singing style remained primarily Inspirational, in the following years she branched out into other forms of musical expression, including Black Gospel, Southern Gospel, classic and modern pop, and musical theatre.

 Listen to Sandi Patty singing

Rich Mullins (1955 - 1997) wrote the classic praise and worship song "Awesome God." Brought up in a Quaker household, he toured with the band Zion in the 1970s. During this time he wrote the song "Sing Your Praise to the Lord," which was subsequently recorded by both Amy Grant and Debby Boone.

Mullins pursued a solo career during the 1980s, before gaining a bachelor's degree in Music Education. This enabled him to teach music to the children of a Navajo Indian reservation in New Mexico. His motivation was to demonstrate Jesus' love for the poor and broken-hearted.

In 1997, Mullins, who greatly respected St. Francis of Assisi, teamed up with Beaker and Mitch McIver to write a musical about the saint's life, called *Canticle of the Plains*. Later that year, he was killed in a motor vehicle accident on his way to a charity concert in Kansas.

 "Awesome God"
"Step by Step (Sometimes by Step)"

Amy Grant (born 1960)

Amy Grant recorded her first album for Myrrh when she was 16 years old. The album contained seven of her own songs. A meteoric rise to fame followed, funded in part by her father, who was a doctor. The title track for her 1979 album *My Father's Eyes* became a number one hit, while her 1982 album *Age to Age* became the first Christian album to go platinum (sell a million copies). This album, described by Howard and Streck as "lite gospel,"[105] contained the signature track "El Shaddai."

In the mid-1980s, Grant toured with up-and-coming singer/songwriter Michael W. Smith and sang backup for Bill Gaither. Later in the 1980s and 1990s, she crossed over to sing secular pop songs.

This move disappointed some of her fans and raised once again the controversial issue of whether it was right for Christian artists to sing mainstream secular material. Those who opposed this argued that Christians were supposed to be "in the world but not of the world" (John 17; see also 1 John 2:15-16). Those in favour pointed out the opportunity for Christian witness to non-Christians. They were also of the opinion that most Christians would have no problem excelling in secular sports teams. Of course, the whole issue was, and still is, one of motivation and heart condition. Each artist needs to examine his or her own heart condition.

Interwoven with this debate is the whole question of entertainment versus ministry. Keith Green was one performer who definitely saw his calling in terms of ministry, but others have looked upon themselves as entertainers, believing that it is better for an audience to be watching a family-friendly concert than other more worldly alternatives.

Listen to Amy Grant singing "El Shaddai" (written by Michael Card)

Michael W. Smith (born 1957)

One of Sandi Patty's most famous songs was "How Majestic Is Your Name," composed by a young Michael W. Smith.

Michael W. Smith, 2014

---

[105] Jay R. Howard and John M. Streck, *Apostles of Rock: The Splintered World of Contemporary Christian Music*, The University Press of Kentucky, Lexington, 1999, p. 62.

Smith became a Christian at the age of ten, but drifted towards substance abuse after leaving high school. A breakdown in 1979 led him to recommit his life to Christ. After that, he toured with the band Higher Ground, while writing songs for artists such as Sandi Patty, Bill Gaither, Kathy Troccoli and Amy Grant. This led to a role as keyboardist, and, eventually, opening act, for Amy Grant's *Age to Age* tour. He was a "teen idol and one-man boy band," purveying a type of music that Don Cusic calls "Gospop – high energy music with a moral message – played by a musician with a mission."[106]

In 1983, he recorded his first album, *The Michael W. Smith Project*, on the Reunion Records label.[107] This album contained the songs "Great Is the Lord" and "Friends," written by Smith and his wife Debbie.

Smith recorded some mainstream albums during the 1990s, before returning to CCM with three live worship albums in the 2000s. His 2008 album, *A New Hallelujah*, featured The African Children's Choir. In 2014, he and Amy Grant were honoured as "cornerstones of Christian music" by the American Society of Composers, Authors and Publishers (ASCAP).

In recent years, Smith has written many songs that have been sung in churches worldwide. These include "Agnus Dei," "Healing Rain," "A New Hallelujah" and "Grace." He has also covered songs such as "Here I Am to Worship" (by Tim Hughes), "Above All" (Paul Baloche and Lenny LeBlanc), "Step by Step" (Beaker aka David Strasser), "Breathe" (Marie Barnett), "Ancient Words" (Lynn DeShazo), and "Open the Eyes of My Heart" (Paul Baloche).

Smith is also a member of CompassionArt, a charity founded by Martin Smith from the band Delirious? Michael W. Smith co-operated with other famous Christian artists to produce an album in 2008, the proceeds of which went to relieve global suffering. He said of the project: "The time spent writing and recording these songs was one of the highlights of my life, and my hope is

---

[106] Cusic, *op.cit.*, pp. 343-44.
[107] Reunion Records had been founded the previous year by Amy Grant's managers Dan Harrell and Mike Blanton.

that these songs on the CompassionArt album will help feed the poor, satisfy the needs of the oppressed and reach out to the downtrodden."[108]

Smith's wife Debbie has co-authored a number of his songs. The couple have five children and reside in Nashville. Smith is the founding pastor of New River Fellowship in Franklin, Tennessee, where he was the lead pastor from 2006 to 2008. Smith and his wife remain involved members of the church.

 Sing or listen to songs written or popularised by Michael W. Smith

"Friends"

"Great Is the Lord"

"Agnus Dei"

"Breathe"

"Above All"

"Ancient Words"

"Here I Am to Worship"

"Open the Eyes of My Heart"

During the 1980s, artists such as Bill Gaither, Andrae Crouch, Debby Boone, Amy Grant, Sandi Patty, Michael W. Smith, Steve Green, John Michael Talbot and Scott Wesley Brown sometimes recorded songs that became classics of praise and worship (much in the vein of the praise/Scripture choruses of the sixties and seventies). These were mellower, more middle-of-the-road songs, often well adapted to congregational singing. Some even found their way into modern church hymnals.

"Thy Word," by Michael W. Smith and Amy Grant, was a good example of 1980s praise and worship, as were songs such as "We Bow Down," "When I Look into Your Holiness," "He Is Exalted" and "We Will Glorify" by Twila Paris. Other well-known praise and worship songs of this era included "As the Deer" (Martin Nystrom), "Fear Not" (Phil Pringle), "The Lord is My Light" (Walt Harrah), "This Is Holy Ground" (Christopher Beatty), "I Stand in Awe," (Mark Altrogge), "You

---

108 Chine Mbubaegbu, "Meet Mr and Mrs Smith," *Idea Magazine*, May 2, 2011, <http://www.eauk.org/idea/meet-mr-and-mrs-smith.cfm>.

Are My Hiding Place" (Michael Ledner) and "Be Still for the Presence of the Lord" (David Evans).[109] Many of these songs were published and recorded by Maranatha! Music.

Sing or listen to one or more of the praise and worship songs mentioned above.

The Catholics

The Second Vatican Council of 1962 – 65 introduced reforms to the liturgy that freed music from the restrictions of the past and introduced the vernacular into church services. No longer was plainsong *de rigueur*. Composers were free to use more contemporary forms of worship, and the laity was encouraged to take a more active part in the Masses, after centuries of clerical domination.

New "folk masses" were written in the mid 1960s, with simple vernacular liturgies. These included *Mass for Young Americans*, by Ray Repp, *Mass of Light*, by David Haas, and *Bread of Life Mass*, by Jeremy Young.

Most influential of all was a group of Jesuits from the seminary at the St. Louis University. This group, known as the "St. Louis Jesuits," wrote and recorded a number of contemporary Christian songs, some of which entered into Catholic hymnals, such as the 1987 *Glory and Praise*.

As the Charismatic Renewal swept through the Catholic Church, worship came to resemble that of the Pentecostal churches. Yet, this growth remained largely invisible to the Protestant Contemporary Christian Music scene. Only occasionally did Catholic artists, such as John Michael Talbot, reach both markets.[110]

---

[109] In 2005, "Be Still for the Presence of the Lord" was voted number six in a BBC *Songs of Praise* favourite hymns survey.

[110] Talbot was born into a Methodist family in 1954. After a spiritual pilgrimage, which led him into the Jesus Movement, he converted to Catholicism and became a third order Franciscan monk in 1978.

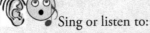Sing or listen to:
A song by the St. Louis Jesuits
An extract from one of the masses mentioned above
A song by John Michael Talbot

Resource Christian Music

Australians Dennis and Nolene Prince initially compiled a number of new praise and worship songs for use in their Melbourne church, the Christian Resource Centre (now known as Kingston City Church). Resource Christian Music was formed in 1981. In many ways, it paralleled New Zealand's Scripture in Song of the previous decade. Since then, RCM has published many compilations of praise and worship songs, in both written and digital formats. Dennis has also written a number of books, including *Worship is a Bowl of Noodles, or What Would Jesus Sing?*

Nolene has a Music degree from Melbourne University, and has written a number of praise and worship songs, including the famous "Holy Is the Lord of Hosts," which has been translated into many different languages.[111]

 "Holy Is the Lord of Hosts"

---

[111]   For the story of how this song came to be written, see <http://www.resource.com.au>.

CHAPTER FIFTEEN

THE BRITISH CONTRIBUTION

Much of the impetus behind modern praise and worship music and hymnody has come from the United Kingdom, with artists and composers such as Graham Kendrick, Stuart Townend, Keith Getty, Robin Mark and Matt Redman.

Graham Kendrick (born 1950)

Graham Kendrick began his career as a member of the Christian beat group Whispers of Truth. His first solo album, recorded in 1971, was *Footsteps on the Sea*. During the 1970s he ministered with Youth for Christ.

He was a co-founder of the 1986 British March for Jesus, which later spread right across the world.[112] The following year he released his signature song "Shine, Jesus Shine."[113] He has written hundreds of other songs. Stuart Townend has called him one of the UK's greatest hymn writers.[114]

Kendrick is also a member of CompassionArt.

---

[112] The original March for Jesus took place in Melbourne, Australia in 1983. It was organised by the Festival of Light. Approximately 7,000 took part and the March finished at the Myer Music Bowl with a victory celebration.

[113] Voted number ten in the 2005 BBC survey.

[114] Stuart Townend, "Songs of Praise – Top 10 Hymns," Archived October 3, 2009, <https://web.archive.org/web/20091003230232/http://www.stuarttownend.co.uk/resources/articles/songs-of-praise-top-10-hymns>.

"Shine, Jesus Shine"
"Heaven Is in My Heart"
"The Servant King"
"Teach Me to Dance"
"Knowing You, Jesus"

Stuart Townend (born 1963)

Stuart Townend, by his own admission, has sought to put theology back into his lyrics. "I think content is vitally important to our corporate worship," [he] shares. "Sometimes great melodies are let down by indifferent or clichéd words. It's the writer's job to dig deep into the meaning of Scripture and express in poetic and memorable ways the truth he or she finds there. Knowing the truth about God and who we are in Him is central to our lives as believers. Songs remain in the mind in a way sermons do not, so songwriters have an important role and a huge responsibility."[115]

Over the past twenty years, he has written some of the great modern hymns of the Christian church, including "In Christ Alone" (co-written with Keith Getty in 2002)[116], "How Deep the Father's Love for Us," "Beautiful Saviour" and "The King of Love." In 2006, he collaborated with Keith Getty in writing the songs for an album based on *The Apostles' Creed*.

Townend is the son of a Church of England vicar. He started learning the piano at age 7 and began writing songs at age 22. He is married with three children.

---

[115] Debra Akins, "Song Story: In Christ Alone," Crosswalk.com, 22 July 2004, <http://www.crosswalk.com/church/worship/song-story-in-christ-alone-1275127.html>

[116] In 2006, "In Christ Alone" hit number one on the United Kingdom Christian Copyright Licensing International (CCLI) charts. In 2010, it was voted second best hymn of all time in a BBC *Songs of Praise* survey.

"In Christ Alone"
"How Deep the Father's Love for Us"
"Beautiful Saviour"

Keith Getty (born 1974)

Keith Getty is another composer who has sought to re-invent the traditional hymn form. His songs, many of them co-written with his wife Kristyn or with Stuart Townend, cross the genres of traditional, classical, folk and contemporary composition. They are featured in modern church hymnals and sung around the world.

Getty was born in Northern Ireland and learnt to play the classical guitar and the flute at a young age. From 1980 to 2001, he orchestrated over 200 projects, including Michael W. Smith's album *Healing Rain*. Since 2001, he has written many hymns and toured widely. His Irish Christmas tour has become an annual event.

To further expand the modern hymn movement, the Gettys have created the Getty Music record label (distributed by Capitol Christian Distribution). In 2017, the inaugural Getty Music Global Conference on worship, the arts, and congregational singing was held in Nashville, Tennessee.

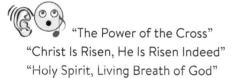 "The Power of the Cross"
"Christ Is Risen, He Is Risen Indeed"
"Holy Spirit, Living Breath of God"

Robin Mark (born 1957)

Robin Mark is another Christian singer/songwriter from Northern Ireland. Although active from the early 1990s, he was little known in the USA and Australia until the release of his signature album, *Revival in Belfast*, in 1999

(Integrity Music). This album contained the well-known songs "Days of Elijah," "Revival" (with Dickey Betts) and "Jesus, All for Jesus."

Mark's follow-up album, *Come, Heal This Land,* went straight to number one on the Christian Retail chart in America. This was the first time that an artist from the UK had achieved this feat.[117]

Mark has recorded thirteen albums with international sales of over two million. He is married with three grown-up children, and is worship leader in his home church – Christian Fellowship Church (CFC) - in East Belfast.

 "Days of Elijah"

"Revival"

"Jesus, All for Jesus"

Matt Redman (born 1974)

Growing up in a dysfunctional family, Matt Redman accepted Christ as his Saviour at the age of ten, under the preaching of Luis Palau. As a teenager, he led worship at an Anglican church in Chorleywood, where Mike Pilavachi was a youth leader. Pilavachi and Redman went on to found Soul Survivor youth festivals in 1993.[118] A Soul Survivor Church was also established in Watford, Hertfordshire.

"Heart of Worship"

The song "Heart of Worship" has become a favorite in churches all over the world, much to the surprise of its composer, Matt Redman.

---

[117] *Cross Rhythms,* 1 September 2001, <http://www.crossrhythms.co.uk/articles/news/Worship_Hit/30919/p1/>

[118] Soul Survivor festivals are still an annual event in the UK and have spread to other parts of the world, including the USA, Australia and New Zealand.

To all intents and purposes, Soul Survivor Church was a world leader in innovative worship in the 1990s. Yet Pastor Mike Pilavachi was concerned that the members of the congregation had become spectators rather than active participants. He therefore made the radical decision to do away with the sound system and the band for a season. "What are you bringing as your offering to God, when you come through the doors on a Sunday?" he asked.

To begin with it was a struggle, and there were some embarrassing silences. Some left the church. Eventually, however, the people found a new voice to express a cappella worship, prayer and prophecy, and the sound system and musicians were re-introduced.

Redman wrote the song in his bedroom as an expression of what he had learned through this experience. He never intended it to be made public, but his pastor encouraged him, and the song featured on his 1999 album *Heart of Worship*.

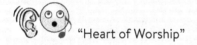 "Heart of Worship"

In 2008, Redman, along with his wife Beth and their three children, moved to Atlanta, Georgia, to help plant a church with Louie Giglio and Chris Tomlin called Passion City Church. They have since returned to England and joined St. Peter's Church in Brighton. Their family has expanded to five children.

In 2011, Redman joined Chris Tomlin, Louie Giglio, and Nathan and Christy Nockels at LIFT – A Worship Leader Collective. His 2011 live album, *10,000 Reasons* was recorded during this event. The title track from the album went to number one on the *Billboard* Christian Songs chart, where it stayed for 13 weeks. It also won two Grammy Awards and a Dove Award in 2013.[119]

---

[119] The two Grammys were for Best Contemporary Christian Music Song and Best Gospel/Contemporary Christian Music Performance. The Dove Award was for Song of the Year.

Redman has written many other well-known songs that have been covered by artists such as Michael W. Smith, Rebecca St. James, Chris Tomlin and Hillsong United. He has also authored a number of books on worship. He is a member and trustee of CompassionArt, and is actively involved in The A21 Campaign to fight human trafficking. His wife, Beth, was one of the founders of the Campaign.

He features regularly in Louie Giglio's Passion Conferences (and records with the associated sixstepsrecords record label).

 "10,000 Reasons (Bless the Lord)" (co-written with Jonas Myrin)
"Blessed Be Your Name"
"Let Everything That Has Breath"
"Better Is One Day"

Delirious?

Delirious? were an English band that operated between 1997 and 2009. Its members comprised Martin Smith (vocals and guitar), Stu G (Stuart Garrard – guitar and backing vocals), Jon Thatcher (bass guitar), Tim Jupp (keys and piano) and Stew Smith (drums and percussion). In their final two years, Paul Evans took over on the drums.

Originally known as The Cutting Edge Band (1992 - 96), the decision to transition to full-time music ministry as Delirious? came about as the result of a near fatal car accident involving Smith and his wife Anna, and band member Jon Thatcher. Smith spent two weeks in hospital, and God planted the vision for the band's future in his heart.

The band is best known for its modern worship songs "Rain Down," "Majesty (Here I Am)," "Lord You Have My Heart," "Thank You for Saving Me," "Did You Feel the Mountains Tremble," "Shout to the North," "What A Friend I've Found" and "I Could Sing of Your Love Forever."

During their career, Delirious? played in over 40 countries around the world. They toured extensively in the United Kingdom, the United States of America,

Europe and India. They also made appearances at the Parachute Music Festival in New Zealand. Their final performance took place in London on 29 November 2009.

Martin Smith and his wife have six children. They founded the charity CompassionArt, largely as a result of Smith's experiences while touring in India. Both Smith and his wife have recently written autobiographies of their experiences as rockstar and stay-at-home mum.

 "Majesty (Here I Am)"
"Did You Feel the Mountains Tremble?"
"Shout to the North"
"I Could Sing of Your Love Forever"

Prom Praise

In 1972, Noël Tredinnick (born 1949) was appointed Organist and Director of Music at the All Souls Church, Langham Place, in the heart of the West End of London: a post he still holds. He founded the All Souls Orchestra on the instruction of the then Rector, hymn writer Michael Baughen, to complement the existing choir and provide an opportunity for Christian musicians to exercise their talent in an orchestral setting. Tredinnick has since conducted the orchestra at many important Christian events, services and festivals in the UK and internationally. The orchestra provides uplifting accompaniments to hymns and popular songs, as well as performing classical works in a Christian context.

The first Prom Praise concert took place at All Souls in October 1977. It contained a familiar mixture of orchestral repertoire, music for solo vocalists, and lots of audience participation. In 1988, the concert moved to its present location in the Royal Albert Hall. The 30th anniversary Prom Praise concert took place in 2007. It was recorded on DVD and featured Stuart Townend and other soloists. The 40th anniversary of the All Souls

Orchestra was held in 2012. Graham Kendrick and Keith and Kristyn Getty were featured performers, along with bass baritone Jonathan Veira.

 Watch a Prom Praise performance.

CHAPTER SIXTEEN

ENTERING THE NEW MILLENNIUM

Steven Curtis Chapman (born 1962)

Since the late 1980s, Steven Curtis Chapman has been recognised as one of the leaders of the Contemporary Christian Music genre. He has released over 20 albums and won five Grammy Awards. His 58 GMA Dove Awards and seven Artist of the Year Dove Awards (as of 2017) are both industry records.

Steven Curtis Chapman

Chapman was born in Paducah, Kentucky. He enrolled in college as a pre-med student, but soon dropped out and went to Nashville to practise music. After having his song "Built to Last" recorded by The Imperials, Chapman was signed by Sparrow Records. His first album, *First Hand* was released in 1987.

In 1992, Chapman transitioned to a more mainstream audience with his album *The Great Adventure*. In 2006, he toured several Asian and Pacific nations, including Australia, New Zealand and China. The following year, he co-headlined Newsong's annual Winter Jam Tour with Jeremy Camp. He used his sons' band,

Colony House, as his backing band. In 2015, his song "Warrior" became the official song for the soundtrack of the Kendrick brothers' movie *War Room*.

Chapman and his wife Mary Beth, are advocates for adoption and they have founded an organisation called Show Hope to assist orphans in the United States and overseas. They have also written children's books with an adoption theme. Of their six children, three are biological and three are adopted Chinese.

In 2008, the youngest adoptee, Maria Sue Chunxi Chapman was killed in a driveway accident. Out of this tragedy, Chapman recorded his seventeenth album *Beauty Will Rise* as a personal tribute to his daughter. Mary Beth also wrote a book called *Choosing to SEE: A Journey of Struggle and Hope*. In 2009, Show Hope finished construction of Maria's Big House of Hope in China. This facility caters for orphans with special needs.

Chapman has also been involved with youth violence prevention, with the international charity World Vision, and with child welfare work in Uganda. He is also a member of CompassionArt. In 2003, he starred in the film *Christmas Child*.

 "His Strength Is Perfect" (with Jerry Salley)
"Warrior"

Rebecca St. James (born 1977)

Rebecca St. James was born Rebecca Smallbone. She spent the first 14 years of her life in Sydney, Australia, before moving with her family to Nashville.

She was only 12 years old when she opened shows for Carman during his Australian tour. Just before moving to the USA, she recorded an independent album *Refresh My Heart*.

Her first major recording, released by Forefront Records in 1994, featured her new stage name Rebecca St. James. Following albums *God* and *Pray* both became RIAA certified Gold. *Pray* also won a Grammy Award in 1999 for Best Rock Gospel Album. Since then there have been four more studio albums, featuring songs such as "Wait for Me," "Reborn," "Song of Love," "I Thank You," "Alive" and "Shine Your Glory Down."

St. James has written a number of books and starred in a rock musical stage show called *iHero* and a number of films, including *Sarah's Choice*, *Suing the Devil* and *Faith of Our Fathers*. She has also achieved fame as a strong pro-life advocate and supporter of sexual purity.

In 2011, she married Jacob "Cubbie" Fink, former bass guitarist for the group Foster the People. Their daughter Gemma was born in 2014.

 Listen to Rebecca St. James

dc Talk

dc Talk. Kevin Max, Toby McKeehan and Michael Tait.

The band dc Talk was formed by Toby McKeehan, Michael Tait and Kevin Max at Lynchburg, Virginia, in 1987. DC Talk is an acronym for "Decent Christian Talk."

The Encyclopedia of Contemporary Christian Music named them "the most popular overtly Christian act of all time."[120]

They released five major studio albums together: *DC Talk* (1989), *Nu Thang* (1990), *Free at Last* (1992), *Jesus Freak* (1995) and *Supernatural* (1998). These albums transitioned from hip hop to a more pop rock style. The albums won a number of Grammy and Dove Awards.

In 2000, the band went into recess, although it has never officially disbanded. There have been reunions since then, and several songs have been recorded. In 2017, the group hosted a reunion cruise.

Toby McKeehan has since performed and recorded as a solo artist under the stage name TobyMac. Michael Tait played the main character in the musical *iHero* before taking over the lead singer role in the Australian band Newsboys. Newsboys performed the title song in the movie *God's Not Dead*. Kevin Max has continued a solo career, although he did spend a short time as lead singer with the band Audio Adrenaline.

"Heaven Bound" - dc Talk
"God's Not Dead" - Newsboys

The 2000s

By the dawn of the twenty-first century, most Pentecostal churches had embraced Contemporary Christian Music. For evangelical churches, the so-called "worship wars" continued to rage. Many solved the dilemma by using "blended worship" – where both contemporary and traditional worship forms were used in services. Where this was not successful, churches held two services – one traditional and the other contemporary. Some churches that had opted for only the "latest and the greatest" of CCM missed out completely on

---

[120] Mark Allan Powell, *Encyclopedia of Contemporary Christian Music*, Hendrickson Publishers, Peabody, Massachusetts, 2002, pp. 239–42.

the vast treasury of "psalms, hymns and spiritual songs" passed down through the ages in the heritage of the Christian church.

Most Contemporary Christian artists defended their music as a means of reaching the unsaved with the Gospel of Jesus Christ. In fact, however, the majority of recordings were purchased and played by Christians and the definition of a "successful" song had more to do with sales volume than souls won. CCM recording artist, Steve Camp, who "has no qualms with naming names and pointing fingers,"[121] was concerned enough about the commercialisation of worship to write:

Those of us who are privileged to represent our Lord Jesus Christ in the arts should be galvanized by mission, not by ambition; by mandate, not by accolades; by love for the Master, not by the allurements of this world. ....Music is a powerful tool from the Lord Jesus to his church intended for worship, praise, encouragement, edification, evangelism, teaching and admonishing. And exhorting God's people to holiness – with always our chief aim 'to glorify God and worship Him forever'. But beloved, the serpentine foe of compromise has invaded the camp through years of specious living, skewed doctrine and most recently secular ownership of Christian music ministries.[122]

"They [Christian recording companies] have all been bought out by secular companies because they see a growing, lucrative market," explained Chris Cole. "So a heavy price is paid – not by the record executives or artists – but by young people buying and absorbing the music. Money is winning over spiritual content, which is being diluted."[123]

The heart of the problem was, once again, the age-old tension between ministry and entertainment. "When worship becomes entertainment, and those

---

[121] Howard and Streck, *op. cit.*, p. 70.
[122] Steve Camp, "Steve Camp's 107 Theses: A Call to Reformation in the Contemporary Christian Music Industry," January 24, 2003. <http://www.worship.com/steve_camp_107_theses.htm>
[123] Chris Cole, "Facing the Music," *IDEA Magazine*, Evangelical Alliance, Spring 2001.

that lead us in worship become performers and icons, then the gospel has been done a great disservice."[124]

The shallowness of the lyrics, the emphasis of style over content, the relegation of theology and doctrine were all worrying trends for some Christians (see Stuart Townend). Michael Baughen, ex-rector of All Souls Church in London, commented, "In these last 40 years there has been a flood of Christian song-writing and a plethora of music groups. The best worship leaders have kept Christ at the centre, rather than themselves; they have seen that words matter more than music; they have kept a balance between good newer songs, older songs, newer hymns and older hymns … reaching across the generations. … They truly understand the place of singing in worship. The worst have eliminated the old (or kept just a few well-worn oldies for they know no others) and have shown no discernment about the new, so that one can be inflicted with a string of 'I', 'Me', 'feeling' songs, often with weak music to weak words."[125]

While some lamented the commercialisation of Christian music, others acknowledged the positive benefits.

First there was consolidation. This affected retail outlets. Large retail chains (such as The Family Bookstore in the USA and Koorong in Australia) were not prejudiced against any particular type of music. They were prepared to stock whatever sold. Consolidation of recording labels also brought a much greater level of expertise into the marketing of Christian product.

It also brought in immense capitalisation. As Don Cusic points out, "Small companies usually cannot afford to have a big hit."[126] The costs of manufacturing, marketing and promoting a new artist before there is any income generation can be prohibitive for small organisations. It is probably true that many Christian artists today would not have had the same success without the financial backing of large companies.

---

[124] Adam Sparks, "Beyond the Worship Wars: Music and Worship in the 21st Century Evangelical Church," *The Theologian*, 2005. <http://www.theologian.org.uk/pastoralia/beyondworshipwars.html>

[125] Michael Baughen, "40 Years On …," *Prom Praise Concert Programme*, April 21, 2012.

[126] Cusic, *op. cit.*, p. 382.

Another positive development was the use of modern computer technology. *Billboard*, the major trade magazine in the music industry began to use SoundScan technology to compile its charts. This was based on bar code readings that showed what music was selling and where. SoundScan clearly showed that gospel music was a very marketable product. This encouraged even the large retail chains, such as Target, Kmart and Wal-Mart, to expand their Christian music retail space. As early as 1995, Christian music was sixth in popularity amongst music genres in the USA (behind rock, country, urban contemporary, pop and rap).

Hillsong

Even in its home country of Australia, the Hillsong Church has divided Christians. Unashamedly contemporary, it has carved a niche for itself worldwide with anointed songs and singers. At the same time, it has received condemnation for being too performance-oriented. David Roark notes that Hillsong "has not only affected the content of the modern evangelical worship service with its songs, but it has also affected the shape of the modern evangelical worship service with its forms."[127]

Pastor Brian Houston and his wife, Bobbie, arrived in Australia (from New Zealand) in 1978. They joined the Sydney Christian Life Centre, which was then being pastored by Brian's father, Frank Houston. In 1983, they formed their own church, known as Hills Christian Life Centre because of its location in the Sydney suburb of Baulkham Hills. The initial congregation numbered 45. Today, Hillsong churches operate in 14 countries and claim to welcome some 100,000 worshippers every week.

In the early 1990s, praise and worship recordings from the Hills Christian Life Centre were released under the name Hillsong. That name was adopted for the church in 1999.

---

[127] David Roark, "How the Hillsong Cool Factor Changed Worship for Good and for Ill," *Christ and Pop Culture*, April 18, 2016. <https://christandpopculture.com/how-the-hillsong-cool-factor-changed-worship-for-good-and-for-ill>

Hillsong was affiliated with the Australian Christian Churches (Assemblies of God) denomination until 2108, when it left to form its own denomination. It runs many different ministries, including Hillsong City Care and Hillsong International Leadership College. It also runs three major conferences every year.

Hillsong has an internationally recognised music ministry. The first studio album, *Spirit and Truth*, was recorded in 1988, and the first live worship album, *The Power of Your Love*, came out in 1992. Groups such as Hillsong Worship, Hillsong United[128] and Hillsong Young and Free record under the Hillsong Music label. Since conception, Hillsong Music has sold over 11 million units worldwide and achieved more than 30 gold and platinum sales awards.

In 2018, the song "What a Beautiful Name", written by Ben Fielding and Brooke Fraser Ligertwood, won a Grammy Award for the Best Contemporary Christian Music Performance/Song.

Geoff Bullock (born 1955) was Hillsong's worship pastor and convenor of conferences between 1987 and 1995. He wrote most of the songs for the early albums, including "The Power of Your Love," "Just Let Me Say," "The Heavens Shall Declare" and "The Great Southland of the Holy Spirit."

 "The Power of Your Love"

Darlene Zschech

Darlene Zschech (born Steinhardt 1965) took over as worship pastor in 1995, and continued in that role until 2007.

During this time, she served as producer, vocal producer or executive producer for more than 20 albums under the Hillsong Music label and wrote more than 80 published worship songs. Under Zschech's leadership, the album *People Just Like Us* (1994) was the first Christian album in Australia to go Gold as well as the first to go Platinum, and the album *For All You've Done*

---

[128]   Hillsong United started in 1998 as part of Hillsong's youth ministry.

(2004) debuted at number one on the Australian Record Industry Association (ARIA) album charts.

Zschech's most famous song is "Shout to the Lord" (1993). The song grew out of a period of struggle and discouragement, but it went on to become one of the most widely-used songs of the Christian church. It is estimated that it has been sung by 25-30 million church-goers every Sunday.[129]

Darlene Zschech has written many other songs, including "God Is in the House," "The Potter's Hand," "Worthy Is the Lamb" and "Victor's Crown."

In 2000, Zschech received a Dove Award nomination for Songwriter of the Year and received the International Award for influence in praise and worship.

Zschech started her singing career at the age of ten, appearing on an Australian television children's show called *Happy Go Round*. Later in her life, she sang jingles for international companies such as McDonalds, KFC and Coca-Cola. Today she speaks openly about issues that have impacted her life, starting with her parent's divorce and her struggle with bulimia. Later, in 2000, she had a miscarriage at twelve weeks. Then in 2013-14 she battled breast cancer, and saw God move in a miraculous way. Through all these trials, she has learned the power of worship. As she said in a 2001 interview, "God wants our worship. He wants our time. But more than anything else, God wants our heart—in good times and bad. I've learned the power of that truth firsthand."[130]

Since 2011, Darlene Zschech and her husband Mark have been senior pastors of Hope Unlimited Church on the Central Coast of New South Wales. They have three girls. Zschech has written a number of books on the subject of worship and is also a member of CompassionArt. It was during a Compassion trip to Central Africa in 2004 that the Zschechs were prompted to initiate Hope Rwanda: 100 Days of Hope, in response to the 1994 genocide that saw up to one million Tutsi tribes people massacred by Hutu government forces. Hope: Rwanda has since expanded to Hope: Global, working in Rwanda, Uganda, Kenya and Cambodia.

---

[129] "Shout to the Lord by Darlene Zschech," *Songfacts*, 2017. <http://www.songfacts.com/detail.php?id=11164>

[130] Camerin Courtney, "The Power of Praising God," *Today's Christian Woman*, March 2001, <http://www.todayschristianwoman.com/articles/2001/march/3.36.html?start=6>.

 "Shout to the Lord"
"Worthy Is the Lamb"
"Victor's Crown"

Reuben Morgan (born 1975) took over as Hillsong's worship pastor in 2008, after Darlene Zschech. He is currently worship pastor of Hillsong London, where he resides with his wife, Sarah, and three children. Morgan has written many of the most famous songs, including "I Give You My Heart," "My Redeemer Lives," "This Is Our God," "Look to the Son" (with Joel Houston, Marty Sampson, Matt Crocker and Scott Ligertwood), "Calvary" (with Jonas Myrin and Mrs Walter G. Taylor) and "Mighty to Save" (with Ben Fielding). "Mighty to Save" won the Worship Song of the Year at the 40th GMA Dove Awards in 2009.

 "Mighty to Save"
"I Give You My Heart"
My Redeemer Lives"

Marty Sampson (born 1979) is another prolific Hillsong writer. His compositions include "God Is Great," "Take It All" (with Matt Crocker and Scott Ligertwood), "Came To My Rescue" (with Joel Davies and Dylan Thomas) and "Saviour King" (with Mia Fieldes).

 "God is Great"
"Saviour King"

Bethel

Bethel Church began in 1952 as a small group of people meeting in a home in Redding, California. Under the leadership of Pastor Robert Doherty, the decision was made to incorporate the church within the Assemblies of God denomination. Subsequent leaders included Vic Trimmer, Earl Johnson, Val Munson and Ray Larson. Under Ray Larson, the church relocated to its present 28 hectare site.

Bill Johnson became pastor in 1996. With an emphasis upon revival, Johnson has seen the church attendance expand to about 3,000, with a plethora of schools and conferences, including the inner healing ministry Sozo, the School of Supernatural Ministry, School of the Prophets, Bethel Christian School, WorshipU, Open Heavens Conference, Kingdom Culture Conference and Arise-Shine Prophetic Conference.

Bethel Music was birthed in 2009 out of the worship ministry of the local church and, in recent years, it has become a fully-fledged record label and publishing company. Since 2015, worship leaders and songwriters have formed an Artists' Collective. In 2017, the members of the collective were Brian and Jenn Johnson, Jeremy Riddle, Matt Stinton, Leeland, Josh Baldwin, Cory Asbury, Steffany Gretzinger, Amanda Cook, Jonathan Helser, Melissa Helser, Hunter Thompson, Kelly Heiligenthal, Paul McClure, Hannah McClure, Sean Feucht and Kristene Dimarco.

Members have toured both within the United States and overseas, and have released a number of albums, including *Be Lifted High* (2011), *We Will Not Be Shaken* (2015) and *Have It All* (2016).

At the 2016 GMA Dove Awards, members from the Bethel Music Collective were nominated for ten Dove Awards. Of the ten nominations, they won four: *Brave New World*, by Amanda Cook, won Inspirational Album of the Year; *Come Alive*, by Bethel Music Kids, won Children's Album of the Year; "No Longer Slaves," by Jonathan David and Melissa Helser, won Worship Song of the Year; and *Without Words: Synesthesia* won Instrumental Album of the Year.

Songs that have been written or performed by Bethel Music include
"It Is Well"
"Lion and the Lamb"
"This Is Amazing Grace" (by Phil Wickham)

"You're Beautiful" (by Phil Wickham)
"King of My Heart" (by Sarah and John Mark McMillan)
"Deep Cries Out"
"Give Me Jesus" (by Fernando Ortega based on an old Negro Spiritual)
"I Love Your Presence"
"No Longer Slaves"

In 1999, the youth group pastored by Banning Liebscher at Bethel Church launched the first Jesus Culture Conference. The **Jesus Culture Band** grew out of these conferences, under the leadership of Kim Walker-Smith, Melissa How and Chris Quilala. Over the next few years a vision grew to equip, encourage and resource "a new breed of revivalists" which were to (in their own words) "see entire cities saved, campuses revolutionized and nations discipled."[131] The Jesus Culture Band admits to being influenced by Hillsong and Delirious?

 Songs associated with Jesus Culture include
"Dance with Me"
"Holy Spirit"
"Alive"
"One Thing Remains"
"Your Love Never Fails"
"How He Loves Us"
"Rooftops"

Kim Walker-Smith
and Chris Quilala

[131] Tony Cummings, "Jesus Culture: Kim Walker Speaks about the powerful Worship Ministry from California," Cross Rhythms, March 12, 2010, <http://www.crossrhythms.co.uk/articles/music/Jesus_Culture_Kim_Walker_speaks_about_the_powerful_worship_ministry_from_California/38957/p1>.

More Artists

Chris Tomlin (born 1972)

Texan-born Chris Tomlin grew up listening to country music. He came from a musical family and, after accepting Christ as Saviour at the age of nine, he went on to compose his first song, "Praise the Lord," at age 14.

He planned to study physiotherapy, but found himself becoming more involved with youth ministry. After attending Bible study sessions with Louie Giglio, he began to lead worship at a number of Giglio events, culminating in the formation of the Passion Conferences for young college students in 1997.

The sixsteprecords label was formed by Giglio in association with the Passion events. The name 'sixsteprecords' comes from 2 Samuel 6:13. When King David was bringing the Ark of the Covenant up to Jerusalem, the priests who carried the Ark took six steps, and then stopped to offer sacrifices as an act of worship. Giglio and Tomlin have always insisted that worship is more than just singing songs. It is a way of life in which we respond from the heart to who God is and what He is doing. "We're not about putting on a big show," says Tomlin. "We don't want to be rock stars. We're about connecting with people and having a shared experience of coming before God and worshipping Him."[132]

Tomlin recorded his first nationally released album, *The Noise We Make*, in 2001. The following year, he became a pastor at Austin's Stone Community Church. He and his band toured extensively with other acts, such as Rebecca St. James, Steven Curtis Chapman, Delirious? tobymac and Israel Houghton. Tomlin also headlined tours, such as the Indescribable Tour with Matt Redman and Louis Giglio (as speaker).

Tomlin was awarded Male Vocalist of the Year at the 2006, 2007 (along with Artist of the Year), and 2008 GMA Dove Awards. In 2008, he assisted Louie Giglio in the formation of Passion Church, in Atlanta, Georgia, and became one of the worship leaders, a role that he has continued to the present day.

---

[132] *ChristianMusic.com,* <http://www.christianmusic.com/chris_tomlin/chris_tomlin. htm>.

Tomlin's sixth studio album *And If Our God Is For Us . . .* was awarded a Grammy for Best Contemporary Christian Music Album is 2012. The seventh album, *Burning Lights* (2012), was only the fourth Christian album to ever hit No. 1 on the Billboard 200.[133]

In 2013, CBN News reported that Tomlin was the most sung artist in the world.[134]

Songs that Tomlin has written or co-written include "How Great Is Our God" (with Ed Cash and Jesse Reeves), "Jesus Messiah" (with Ed Cash, Daniel Carson and Jesse Reeves), "Our God" (with Matt Redman, Jesse Reeves and Jonas Myrin), "We Fall Down," "Forever," "Holy Is the Lord" (with Louie Giglio) and "Even So Come" (with Jason Ingram and Jess Cates). He has also written new versions of old hymns, such as "Amazing Grace (My Chains Are Gone)" (with Louie Giglio), "Joy to the World (Unspeakable Joy)," (with Ed Cash and Matt Gilder) and "Come Thou Fount (I Will Sing)."

Chris Tomlin is a member of CompassionArt. He and his wife, Lauren, have two daughters (as of 2016).

Sing or listen to songs written or popularised by Chris Tomlin
"Amazing Grace (My Chains Are Gone)"
"How Great Is Our God"
"Our God"
"Forever"
"Good, Good Father" (written by Pat Barrett and Anthony Brown)
"Indescribable" (written by Laura Story)

---

[133] The first Christian No. 1 was Bob Carlisle's "Butterfly Kisses" *(Shades of Grace)* in 1997. The second was LeAnn Rimes' "You Light up My Life" *(Inspirational Songs)*, also in 1997. The third was tobymac's "Eye On It" in 2012.
[134] "Chris Tomlin Most Sung Songwriter in the World," *CBN News*, July 2, 2013, <http://www.cbn.com/cbnnews/us/2013/july/chris-tomlin-most-sung-songwriter-in-the-world/?mobile=false>

Casting Crowns

Casting Crowns, 2013. Members from left to right – Megan Garrett, Brian Scoggin, Chris Huffman, Juan DeVevo, Mark Hall, Hector Cervantes, Melodee DeVevo. Josh Mix has since replaced Hector Cervantes.

Casting Crowns started as a student worship band at First Baptist Church, Daytona Beach, Florida, led by youth pastor Mark Hall. The band relocated to Stockbridge, Georgia, before recording two independent albums. Their first studio album, *Casting Crowns*, was produced for the Beach Street Records label by Mark Miller and Steven Curtis Chapman. The song "Voice of Truth" reached number one on three major Contemporary Christian music charts, *Billboard* and *20 The Countdown Magazine*. It also featured in the trailer and the ending from the Kendrick brothers' film *Facing the Giants*. The album itself was certified platinum in 2005. Another song "Slow Fade," from the album *The Altar and the Door*, was used on the soundtrack of another Kendrick film, *Fireproof*. The lead single "Courageous" from the 2011 album *Come to the Well* was used to promote the film of the same name.

The 2009 album *Until the Whole World Hears* contained the songs "Blessed Redeemer," "Joyful, Joyful" and "Glorious Day (Living He Loved Me)." "Joyful, Joyful" was a modern rendition of Henry Van Dyke's hymn "Joyful, Joyful We Adore" Thee from Beethoven's 9th Symphony. "Glorious Day" was based on a hymn written in 1910 by J. Wilbur Chapman, with verse melody from Michael Bleecker.

In 2009, Casting Crowns was asked to participate in the Spring Friendship Arts Festival in North Korea. This was their second invitation.

Early in 2015, lead singer Mark Hall was diagnosed with kidney cancer. An operation to remove the kidney was successful, and the cancer has been contained.

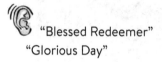
"Blessed Redeemer"
"Glorious Day"

MercyMe

The band MercyMe was formed in 1994. Bart Millard had originally wanted to be a football player, but an injury turned his thoughts towards singing. Millard and a friend, James "Jim" Bryson (keyboard), worked together in a church band in Florida before undertaking a trip to Switzerland. The idea of becoming fulltime musicians originated at this time.

Millard and his friend, guitarist Mike Scheuchzer, moved to Oklahoma City to form MercyMe with Bryson. They set up a studio and "living area" in an abandoned day-care centre. Bassist Nathan Cochran and drummer Robby Shaffer joined the band later on and together they recorded six independent albums.

The name "MercyMe" apparently originated from Millard's grandmother. Concerned that her grandson was home whenever she called, she would exclaim, "Well mercy me, why don't you get a real job?"

In 2001, they signed with INO Records.[135] Their debut album *Almost There* contained the crossover single "I Can Only Imagine." Millard had written this song while thinking about the death of his father. The song elevated the album to double platinum certification (two million sales). "I Can Only Imagine" won two GMA Dove Awards in 2002, for Pop/Contemporary Recorded Song of the Year and Song of the Year. Millard also won Songwriter of the Year. The 2018 movie *I Can Only Imagine* tells Millard's story.

As of 2017, MercyMe has released nine studio albums, two compilation albums, two Christmas albums and two video albums. The group has also had 13 consecutive top five singles on the *Billboard* Christian Songs chart, with seven of them reaching number one.

Guitarist Barry Graul joined the band in 2003, and Jim Bryson left in 2014. In 2009, "The Rock and Worship Roadshow" raised money to help children with juvenile diabetes through Imagine A Cure and those with medical needs around the world through Compassion International.

Bart Millard has also had a solo career, recording two hymn albums *Hymned, No. 1* and *Hymned Again.* He is married to Shannon, and the couple has five children.

 "I Can Only Imagine"

---

135   INO Records is now known as Fair Trade Services. It is owned by David C. Cook and distributed by Sony Music Entertainment.

EPILOGUE

Over the past 60 years, the Christian music scene worldwide has been transformed by the advent of Contemporary Christian Music. Whether this constitutes a revolution or a process of evolution is a debatable point.

In their book *Apostles of Rock*, Jay Howard and John Streck argue for the evolutionary approach. "Contemporary Christian music can be seen as the merging of two distinct musical streams: the safe, acceptable church musics of the evangelical church on the one hand and rock 'n' roll on the other."[136] This is somewhat of a simplification, however, given that rock 'n' roll itself had at least part of its origin in church music – particularly Black Gospel. "Black gospel provided white rock with the style, songs, and artists to imitate."[137] Even Southern Gospel contributed. Elvis Presley was one who was strongly influenced by Southern Gospel groups, particularly the Blackwood Brothers.

Of course, it is virtually impossible to define Contemporary Christian Music, except to say that it is modern music, written and performed by people who hold to the Christian faith. "Standing in the gap between evangelical Christianity on the one side and youth culture on the other, contemporary Christian music offers evangelical Christians who cannot identify with what they see on MTV their own set of alter egos."[138]

CCM also covers a wide range of musical genres, from the hymnody of Stuart Townend to the hard rock and heavy metal of bands such as Stryper and Whitecross. Wikipedia lists almost 400 Christian rock bands, mainly in the USA, and this list excludes bands that play primarily heavy metal and hardcore punk.[139]

---

[136] Howard and Streck, *op. cit.*, p. 26.

[137] Tim Anderson, "The Roots of Rock: Did Gospel Music Give Birth to the Devil's Rock 'n' Roll?" *Contemporary Christian Magazine*, February 1984, pp. 12-14, 42.

[138] Howard and Streck, *op. cit.*, p. 5.

[139] Accessed 21 June 2017.

In an attempt to bring some understanding of the "splintered world" of CCM, Howard and Streck propose classifying artists in terms of their response to secular culture. They draw heavily on Richard Niebuhr's 1951 work *Christ and Culture*. Niebuhr proposes five approaches for relating Christ to culture. He calls these "Christ against culture," "Christ of culture," "Christ above culture," "Christ and culture in paradox" and "Christ the transformer of culture."

The first group of CCM artists, "Separational CCM," falls into the "Christ against culture" category. Separational CCM artists see themselves as "in the world but not of the world." Their emphasis is on being different, and they are strongly of the persuasion that their music is a "ministry."

From the early days of the Jesus Movement, evangelism was seen as music's *raison d'être*. Bob Hartman, founder of the band Petra, says, "We were totally evangelistic at the beginning; there wasn't a Christian concert scene, per se. The people who would have us in to play were usually people with a burden for the lost. They knew that rock music was a new medium and that it would hold the kids so they would have us come play."[140] The evangelistic thrust was partly motivated by a strong belief in the imminent return of Jesus. This is reflected in the name Maranatha! Music used by Calvary Chapel, Maranatha meaning "the Lord cometh."

The irony of all this is that the majority of young people who purchased albums by CCM artists, or who attended churches or festivals where the music was being performed, were already "born-again" Christians. In a sense, the artists were "preaching to the converted."

As the Jesus Movement began to fade in the mid-1970s, many Separational CCM artists began to view their role as facilitators of praise and worship. Dallas Holm demonstrated this new trend by calling his band Dallas Holm and Praise. Barry McGuire reflected that the task of the musician was to worship God and let Him reach the people.[141] Twila Paris, one of the main composers of praise and worship songs in the 1980s, testified that by their ability to draw a crowd of people, worship songs could be a powerful tool in street evangelism.

---

[140] Quincy Smith-Newcomb, "An Interview with Greg Volz and Bob Hartman of Petra," *Progressive Pacer*, Nov. 1982, pp. 4-7.

[141] Howard and Streck, *op. cit.*, p. 62.

The efficacy of CCM praise and worship songs was reflected in the 1996 survey, done by *Your Church* magazine, which found that a majority of churches in the USA were now using more contemporary forms of worship, and were enjoying much larger attendance figures than the more traditional churches.[142]

As Contemporary Christian Music made more inroads into the established churches, many Separational CCM artists began recording songs of exhortation, in an attempt to nurture and disciple Christians. Keith Green led the way here with hard hitting lyrics that sought to provoke Christians into giving their all to Christ. Even Petra admitted, in relation to their 1987 album *This Means War!* that "Our lyrics seek to edify the body of Christ, and we're not writing songs that are mostly directed to nonbelievers or anything."[143] Incidentally, the name of the album reflected a new enthusiasm for spiritual warfare that pervaded Separational CCM at this time.

"Integrational CCM" falls loosely into Niebuhr's category "Christ in culture." The rationale here is that there is enough good in society to respond to music with wholesome values. From this point of view, Integrational CCM artists regard their music not so much as a ministry, but rather as providing "sanctified entertainment" for both Christians and non-Christians.[144]

Recognising that Contemporary Christian Music was "trapped within the boundaries of an evangelical subculture,"[145] some artists and recording companies sought opportunity to "cross-over" into the mainstream market. Amy Grant and Michael W. Smith were amongst the few who achieved success. They articulated three rationales for their position, the first being, of course, that their music offered a wholesome alternative to mainstream pop.

A second rationale arose out of a perception that it was wrong to try and divide society into sacred and secular spheres. By articulating a Christian worldview, Integrational CCM artists felt that, rather than offering a "watered down gospel," they were providing "a commentary on everyday life from a Christian

---

[142] *Ibid.*, p. 63.
[143] Brian Quincy Newcomb, "Petra's Battle," *Contemporary Christian Music*, Oct. 1987.
[144] John W. Styll, "Editor's Comment: Amy Grant's Sanctified Entertainment," *Contemporary Christian Music*, July-August 1986, p. 4.
[145] Howard and Streck, *op. cit.*, p. 78.

perspective."[146] This reasoning also supported the third rationale, that such artists were in a position to be able to witness to those within the secular music industry.

Some Integrational CCM artists wondered why it was necessary to have an ulterior motive for recording music. Couldn't they just make music for the sake of making music? "Transformational CCM" artists have taken this argument to a whole new level.

For them, music is not about either ministry or entertainment; it is about creating an art form. Winning souls or achieving commercial success is only of secondary importance. The God of Transformational CCM artists is not the comforting best friend, praised in simplistic lyrics, yet "disconnected from the Christian experience, disconnected from human experience, disconnected from the outside world."[147] He is "divine, omnipotent, and unfathomable."

This is Niebuhr's Christ the Transformer of Culture. Christ comes to a culture that is "fallen and broken" and seeks to restore it to His original intentions and purposes. Transformational CCM, therefore, explores the darker sides of life in order to move them toward redemption. It is this belief in a redeemable culture that separates Transformational from Separational CCM.

The conflict between separational and transformational music mirrors the differing interpretations of the purpose of art. To the former, art is to be used to communicate the Gospel. Any other purpose is deemed to reflect a luke-warm Christianity. The transformationalists, on the other hand, view art as more an expression of truth. Insofar as art (and music in this case) has aesthetic quality and expresses truth, then it is "good art" and reflects the divine image of God.

As one of the leading advocates of Transformational CCM, Brian Quincy Newcomb encourages Christian artists to "make albums that speak intelligently and relevantly to our world," and that possess "bold, artistic honesty, musical power and cultural edge." In response to Christian artists who say "Jesus gave me this song," Newcomb notes, tongue-in-cheek that perhaps, sometimes, they should have given it back.[148] Steve Scott notes that the very act of *creating*

---

[146] *Ibid.*, p. 101.
[147] *Ibid.*, p. 124.
[148] Brian Quincy Newcomb, "Q Thoughts," *Syndicate*, 1992-93, p. 4.

reflects the fact that we are "created beings reliant upon the grace of a creative God."[149]

In the sense that it focuses on the individual experience of living in a fallen and broken world, Transformational CCM "can at times emerge as the self-conscious and self-important ruminations of individuals trying too hard to claim the title 'artist.'"[150]

It can also be hard to sell. "Expressing the mystery of God may make sense from an artistic standpoint, but it makes little sense from a business standpoint."[151] A number of record labels that sort to market strictly Transformational CCM did not last very long. Others have sort to recast transformational artists in a format that would have wider appeal to evangelical audiences. The New Zealand band Hoi Polloi are a case in point.

Their song lyrics attempted to present personal struggles with life experiences and faith, while, at the same time, "hopefully presenting the underlying theme that despite all this, there's hope through Christ."[152] Signed by American record label Reunion, the members of the band were rebranded as "pop rockers" and the more controversial songs were deleted from their first album (1992). A third album for a new record producer allowed them to return to their transformational roots, but the band disbanded in 1996.

The differences amongst various branches of CCM are really part of an ongoing search for authenticity and relevancy amongst Christian artists. Too often that search boils down to the single question "what sells best?" This question has become even more urgent as the industry has battled with the onset of the digital age.

By 2014, the sale of CCM albums had plummeted from about 50 million to just 17 million. Magazines began to run articles with titles such as "Who Killed

---

[149] Steve Scott, "Scratching the Surface," in Colin Harbison et. al., *Art Rageous*, Cornerstone Press, Chicago, 1992.

[150] Howard and Streck, *op. cit.*, p. 144.

[151] *Ibid.*, p. 189.

[152] Jan Willem Vink, "Hoi Polloi: Music for the Masses Played by New Zealand Pop Rockers." *Cross Rhythms*, February 1, 1993. <http://www.crossrhythms.co.uk/articles/music/Hoi_Polloi_Music_for_the_masses_played_by_New_Zealand_pop_rockers/36878/p1>

the Contemporary Christian Music Industry?"[153] As labels grew wary of taking risks, they turned increasingly to safe worship music – as evidenced by artists such as Chris Tomlin, Matt Redman and Hillsong United. "In CCM, if you want to sing about certain, more uncomfortable things, you won't have an opportunity," says John Mark McMillan.[154]

On the positive side, digital recording tools help many artists record part or all of their albums outside of expensive recording studios. "Artists who become web- and social-networking- savvy can promote their work just as effectively online as any of the major 'Christian' labels seem to do."[155]

In a comparison of modern CCM with traditional American shaped-note singing, Leah Libresco found that, whereas, in shaped-note songs, the subjects of Death, Darkness and Sin were treated equally with Life, Light and Grace, in modern CCM, the lyrics tended overwhelmingly towards the positive.[156]

On the subject of sin, John Wesley wrote, "Before I preach love, mercy, and grace, I must preach sin, law, and judgment." Perhaps it is time for Christian music to "acknowledge the exilic nature of the Church in the world. Here we have no lasting home, so our hymns can have the timbre of exile—the grief, the anger, the wrestling with God, the joy that is fierce and defiant rather than safe and smiley."[157]

In the present youth-orientated culture of much of the Christian church, knowledge of, or interest in, Christian music seldom extends back more than ten years (in some cases less than one year). Churches would do well to start drawing from the whole heritage of Christian music in their worship services. In

---

[153] Tyler Huckabee, "Who Killed the Contemporary Christian Music Industry?" *The Week*, February 17, 2016. <http://theweek.com/articles/555603/who-killed-contemporary-christian-music-industry>

[154] *Ibid.*

[155] Paul D. Race, *A Brief History of Contemporary Christian Music*, <https://schooloftherock.com/html/a_brief_history_of_contemporar.html>. Accessed July 11, 2017.

[156] Leah Libresco, "The Sun Is Always Shining in Modern Christian Pop," *FiveThirtyEight*, June 2, 2016. <https://fivethirtyeight.com/features/the-sun-is-always-shining-in-modern-christian-pop>

[157] Alexi Sargeant, "Songs of Exile," *First Things*, July 6, 2016. <https://www.firstthings.com/blogs/firstthoughts/2016/06/songs-of-exile>

the words of Jesus, "Therefore every scribe who has become a disciple of the kingdom of heaven is like the head of a household, who brings out of his treasure things that are new *and* fresh and things that are old *and* familiar." (Matthew 13:52 Amplified Bible) It is hoped that this book may provide the resources for such a venture of faith.

BIBLIOGRAPHY

Achtemeier, Paul J. (ed.), *Harper's Bible Dictionary*, Harper & Row, San Francisco, 1985.

Anderson, Tim, "The Roots of Rock: Did Gospel Music Give Birth to the Devil's Rock 'n' Roll?" *Contemporary Christian Magazine*, February 1984.

Appleby, David P., *History of Church Music*, Moody Press, Chicago, 1965.

Baker, Paul W., *Contemporary Christian Music: Where It Came from, What It Is, Where It's Going*, Crossway Books, Winchester, Illinois, 1985.

Bartleman, Frank, *How Pentecost Came to Los Angeles: As It Was in the Beginning*, 1925.

Bream, Jon, "Divided Loyalties: Charts Split Gospel Music into Separate Camps," *Minneapolis-St. Paul Star Tribune*, October 27, 1991.

Brown, Robert K. and Norton, Mark R., *The One Year Great Songs of Faith*, Tyndale House Publishers, Wheaton, Illinois, 1995.

Camp, Steve, "Steve Camp's 107 Theses: A Call to Reformation in the Contemporary Christian Music Industry," January 24, 2003.

Chattaway, Peter T., "Billy Graham Goes to the Movies" *Patheos*, August 23, 2005.

Cole, Chris, "Facing the Music," *IDEA Magazine*, Evangelical Alliance, Spring 2001.

Conner, Kevin J., *Restoration Theology*, KJC Publications, Vermont, Victoria, 1998.

Connor, Kevin J., *The Tabernacle of David*, Bible Temple – Conner Publications, Portland, Oregon, 1976.

Courtney, Camerin, "The Power of Praising God," *Today's Christian Woman*, March 2001.

Crosby, Fanny J., *Memories of Eighty Years*, James H. Earle and Co., Boston, 1906.

Cusic, Don, *The Sound of Light: A History of Gospel and Christian Music*, Hal Leonard Corporation, Milwaukee, Wisconsin, 2002.

Darden, Robert, "Remembering Andrae Crouch, Dead at 72," *Christianity Today*, January 8, 2015.

Davis, George T., *Twice around the World with Alexander*, The Christian Herald, New York, 1907.

Dowley, Tim, *Christian Music: A Global History*, Lion Hudson, Oxford, 2011.

Encyclopaedia Britannica, < http://www.britannica.com>.

Eskridge, Larry, *God's Forever Family: The Jesus People Movement in America, 1966-1977*, University of Stirling, Stirling, Scotland, 2005.

Fausset, A. R., *Fausset's Bible Dictionary*, Zondervan, Grand rapids, Michigan, 1949.

Gaither, Bill, *It's More than Music: Life Lessons on Friends, Faith and What Matters Most*, Warner Faith, 2003.

Galiley, Shimon, "Jesus Music: The Story of the Jesus Movement and Evaluation of Its Musical Impact," Senior Honors Thesis, Liberty University, 2011.

Goff, James R., *Close Harmony: A History of Southern Gospel*, University of North Carolina Press, Chapel Hill, 2002.

Gold, Charles E., "The Gospel Song: Contemporary Opinion," *The Hymn*, Vol. 9, No. 3, July 1958.

Graham, Billy, *The Jesus Generation*, Zondervan, Grand Rapids, Michigan, 1971.

Green, Keith, *A Cry in the Wilderness*, Word Publishing, Milton Keynes, 1993.

Howard, Jay R. and Streck, John M., *Apostles of Rock: The Splintered World of Contemporary Christian Music*, The University Press of Kentucky, Lexington, 1999.

Huckabee, Tyler, "Who Killed the Contemporary Christian Music Industry?" *The Week*, February 17, 2016.

Hughes, Charles W., *American Hymns Old and New*, Columbia University Press, New York, 1980.

Jacks Gregory H., "I Want to Be in That Number: A Song Profile of 'When the Saints Go Marching In'," *Syracuse University Honors Program Capstone Project*, Paper 817, 2015.

Libresco, Leah, "The Sun Is Always Shining in Modern Christian Pop," *FiveThirtyEight*, June 2, 2016.

Piggin, Stuart and Linder, Robert, *The Fountain of Public Prosperity*, Monash University Publishing, Clayton, Victoria, Australia, 2018.

Powell, Mark Allan, *Encyclopedia of Contemporary Christian Music*, Hendrickson Publishers, Peabody, Massachusetts.

Race, Paul D., *A Brief History of Contemporary Christian Music*, <https://schooloftherock.com/html/a_brief_history_of_contemporar.html>.

Reich, Charles, *The Greening of America*, Allen Lane The Penguin Press, London, 1971.

Roark, David, "How the Hillsong Cool Factor Changed Worship for Good and for Ill," *Christ and Pop Culture*, April 18, 2016.

Robinson-Martin, Trineice, "Performance Styles and Musical Characteristics of Black Gospel Music," *Journal of Singing*, Vol. 65, No. 5, May/June 2009.

Robinson-Martin, Trineice, "Performance Styles and Musical Characteristics of Black Gospel Music," *Journal of Singing*, Vol. 65, No. 5, May/June 2009.

Sargeant, Alexi, "Songs of Exile," *First Things*, July 6, 2016.

Smith, Jane Stuart and Carlson, Betty, *The Gift of Music: Great Composers and Their Influence*, Crossway Books, Wheaton, 1995.

Smith, John Arthur, "Musical Aspects of Old Testament Canticles in Their Biblical Setting," in Iain Fenlon, ed., *Early Music*, Vol.17, Cambridge University Press, Cambridge, 1998.

Sparks, Adam, "Beyond the Worship Wars: Music and Worship in the 21st Century Evangelical Church," *The Theologian*, 2005.

Stainer, John, *The Music of the Bible*, Novello and Co. Ltd., London, 1914.

The Billy Graham Team, *Crusader Hymns & Hymn Stories*, Minneapolis, Minnesota, 1967.

Thomas, Velma Maia, *No Man Can Hinder Me: The Journey from Slavery to Emancipation through Song*, Crown Publishers, New York, 2001.

Wolfe, Charles K., "Columbia Records and Old-Time Music," *JEMF Quarterly*, pp. 118-125.

Wolfe, Charles K., "'Gospel Boogie': White Southern Gospel Music in Transition, 1945-55," <http://nativeground.com/gospel-boogie-white-southern-gospel-music-transition-1945-55-charles-wolfe/>.

PICTURE CREDITS

Deror avi, p. 7

Peter Pringle, p. 10

John Stainer, *The Music of the Bible,* pp. 11, 13

Lalupa - Creative Commons Licence 3.0, p. 15

Alfred Wesley Wishart, *A Short History of Monks and Monasteries,* 1900, p. 31

Famous Composers and Their Works, Vol. 1, 1906, p. 53

Princeton Theological Seminary Library, p. 58

Illustrated London News, p. 59

Library of Congress, pp. 63, 68, 77, 89, 90, 102, 126, 130, 158

The New York Public Library, The Miriam and Ira D. Wallach Division of Art, Prints and Photographs, p. 66

G. H. Hollister, *The History of Connecticut, from the First Settlement of the Colony to the Adoption of the Present Constitution, 1855,* p. 72

Ed Porter Thompson, *A Youth's History of Kentucky for School and General Reading,* 1897, p. 80

Stereoscopic Co., *Notables of Britain,* c.1897, p. 86

A. Burt, Music, Books, & Stationery - Carte de Visite, p. 94

C. U. Williams, 1908, Joyce Images, p. 104

Princeton Theological Seminary Library, p. 106a

Prints & Photographs Department, MSRC – Deep Roots Magazine, p. 120

IntellectualChristianWikiUser, Creative Commons 4.0 Licence, p. 121

F.N. Broers / Anefo - Nationaal Archief, Creative Commons 3.0. Licence, p. 123a

COLOUR INSERTS

Chris Hansen/Baylor Photography, Photo 24
Barry McGuire, Photo 25
Scott Wesley Brown, Photo 26
Ruth Daniel, Creative Commons 2.0, Photo 27
Graham Kendrick, Make Way Music, Photo 28
Getty Music, Public Domain, Photo 29
Keith and Kristyn Getty, Photo 30
Robin Mark, Photo 31
Labjunkie, Creative Commons licence 3.0, Photo 32
Gordon McKinlay, Creative Commons Licence 2.0, Photo 33
Shannon from Altus, USA - Wait for Me, Creative Commons Licence 2.0, Photo
    34
Matt Malone, Photo 35
Brent Van Auken, Jesus Culture, Photo 36
DeaPeaJay (Flickr user), Creative Commons Licence 2.0, Photo 37
WordyGirl90, Creative Commons Licence 3.0, Photo 38

GENERAL INDEX

SONG AND TUNE TITLE INDEX

ABOUT THE AUTHOR

Mike Spencer is a New Zealander who now lives in Australia. After the death of his first wife, in 2014, he married Christine. Between them, the couple have eight grownup children and a number of step-children. Mike is a teacher by profession. He taught history and geography in state secondary schools for 12 years, then in a Christian school for another 12 years. From 1995 to 2015 he wrote educational resources for Christian schools in Australia, New Zealand and the South Pacific. Mike is the author of the book *One People, One Destiny: A Christian History of Australia*. Best-selling writer and inspirational speaker, Col Stringer, said of this book, "Mike Spencer has produced an excellent and valuable work in his book dealing with our Christian Heritage." Mike has combined his love of music and his love of history in the writing of this present work.

Mike is an entertaining speaker. He is available to talk about Australia's Christian heritage and to run seminars on the history of Christian music. These seminars are interactive, and involve video clips and congregational singing.

Email michaelspencer8@bigpond.com for further information or visit Mike's website www.mikespencer.com.au.

1. Levitical singers and musicians in the Temple courtyard; 2. The blowing of the shofar at the Western Wall in Jerusalem during the eve of Rosh Hashanah; 3. Martin Luther (painting by Lucas Cranach the Elder); 4. Johann Sebastian Bach in a portrait by Elias Gottlob Haussmann; 5. Charles Wesley.

6. Ira Sankey and Fanny Crosby composing a new song. 7. This portable record player uses 78 rpm disks; 8. tobyMac 2015; 9. Jake Hess; 10. James Blackwood; 11. J.D. Sumner; 12. Ernie Haase; 13. Russ Taff

14. Bill and Gloria Gaither, 2016; 15. Stuart Hamblen; 16. George Beverly Shea; 17. John W. Peterson; 18. Pat Boone; 19. Cliff Richard

20. A selection of Gospel Chorus books from the 1950s; 21. Parachute Music Festival, 2010; 22. Scripture in Song record albums.

23. Phil Keaggy; 24. Kurt Kaiser and Ralph Carmichael; 25. Barry McGuire with President Jimmy Carter and his wife Rosalynn; 26. Scott Wesley Brown.

27. Amy Grant and Michael W. Smith performing at the Mabee Center in Tulsa, Oklahoma, USA, in 2011; 28. Graham Kendrick; 29. Stuart Townend.

30. Keith and Kristyn Getty; 31. Robin Mark; 32. Matt Redman in concert, 2010; 33. Delirious? performing in Edinburgh, November 2009; 34. Rebecca St. James, 2007; 35. Inside Hillsong Church, 2007.

36. Jesus Culture 2013. (l to r back - Jeffrey Kunde, Ian McIntosh, Josh Fisher; bench - Skyler Smith, Kim Walker-Smith, Chris Quilala); 37. Chris Tomlin, 2007; 38. Bart Millard and drummer Robby Shaffer performing in 2008.

9 780648 371977